The Greatest School Survival Tips in the World

Essential school survival tips for girls, to see you through years 6 & 7 ... and beyond!

by

Maddie Boyers
aged 13

A 'The Greatest in the World' book

www.thegreatestintheworld.com

Cover design:
Cliff Hayes
www.hayesdesign.co.uk

Layout:
Shazia Saleemi
www.designspirit.co.uk

Illustrations:
Maryam Saleemi

Copy editor:
Bronwyn Robertson
www.theartsva.com

Y373

Series creator/editor:
Steve Brookes

Published in 2009 by
The Greatest in the World Ltd, PO Box 3182,
Stratford-upon-Avon, Warwickshire CV37 7XW

A CIP catalogue record for this book is available from the British Library
ISBN 978-1-905151-49-3

Printed and bound in Italy by Graphicom

A big thank you to my junior school Head Mr Paul Bryan for his sense of humour and massive confidence building ability through his fantastic drama lessons. I will never forget our performance of Joseph at the end of Year 6.

Love and thanks to my godmother Julie Peasgood for continuous support and encouragement to write this book.

Finally, thanks to my Mum and Dad for helping me throughout the process.

This book belongs to

Name: ....

Contents

A few words from Maddie. . .

I started writing this book at the beginning of Year 6. I found it tough to start with but once I got into it, it was a lot easier. All the tips have been written by me from my own personal experiences. Without the encouragement of friends and family I would not have been able to write this book, I would have been out playing hockey instead! Researching and writing it has helped me a lot with many different things from revision and exams to health and general fitness.

From aged 2 I went to the Montessori nursery in Grimsby but can't remember much about this now other than playing with sand and bricks. I then went to St Martin's school when I was 4 and stayed there until the end of Year 4. It was a good school, I enjoyed it and I learnt a lot, especially about discipline and manners and still have friends now from both those places. My parents both worked in Grimsby so it was easy for them to drop me off and pick me up. But then I discovered sport and as a town school St Martin's didn't have a field or many facilities. It was time for a change, but change isn't that easy.

So, when I got to Year 5, I found myself being the new girl at Hymers College Junior School in Hull and I didn't know anyone. When I arrived everybody there already knew everyone else. I was quite scared to start with but everyone was so friendly and the whole school was really welcoming. I am still there today and I love it. What really helped was that I have some great friends.

This book covers so much. I have tried most of these tips myself and I hope that they work for you. Some of them are really daft but fun to try, but most of the tips are quite sensible and will hopefully help you in some way, large or small. Some are just common sense, but you should give them a go, as they might not answer your problem but might give you a similar idea or be good to pass on to your friends or parents.

I am hoping this can be the kind of book that you can read a bit of, put in your bag and pull out when necessary. Even if you only get one good tip from this book I'll know it was worth doing. It has been fun doing it so I hope you have as much fun reading it. No school is the same, so some of the tips won't work for everyone. Remember, school days are the best days of your life, so don't let teachers, other kids or bullies spoil them for you — I hope these tips will help you make the most of them.

Maddie x

chapter 1
Rise & shine

We girls do not talk in class, we distribute vital information!

Saved by the bell

An alarm clock is a must to ensure you never oversleep, because that means big trouble. And the definition of an alarm clock is something that scares the living daylights out of you! They are cheap to buy from about £5 or put it on a birthday or Christmas list. One thing you must remember to do is put your clocks forward in March and back in October as this is one of the main reasons for being late for school (more of this later). A good tip is to get to bed an hour earlier in March. It may only be an hour but you really miss it in the mornings for a couple of days, as it is a lot darker.

Go green

Don't spend ages in the shower. You will have lots more time to eat, look nice and maybe a little longer in bed. It would help you a lot in the mornings; also you would help the environment. Remember for every 2 minutes you spend in the shower you use as much water as a person in Africa uses for everything in their life for a whole day.

Get knotted

Do you knot your tie once a year and slip it over you head every day? If you have to start afresh here's how!

- The wide end should be about 12 inches longer than the narrow end.

- Cross the wide end over the narrow end.

- Bring the wide end around and behind the narrow end.

- Bring the wide end up.

- Pull the wide end through the loop.

- Bring the wide end around the front, over the narrow end from right to left.

- Again bring the wide end up and through the loop.

- Bring the wide end down through the knot front.

- With both hands tighten the knot carefully towards your collar.

Sorted!

Be prepared

You are well advised to follow the famous motto of the Scouts by having your school bags packed before you go to bed for a quick getaway in the morning. No matter what you think, you will never ever have enough time to do everything in the morning. It's better to use early morning time to have a good breakfast (more of that later), brush your teeth and hair, and be pleasant to your parents.

Best back packs

We are all in danger of getting the hump! Seriously, back pain can result from using the wrong rucksacks — usually filled with heavy books and kit. Choose a cool one or customise your own, but aim for one that feels comfy and doesn't ruin your posture. These tips should keep you walking straight and looking good.

- Choose broad straps and an alternative top carry handle to vary the way you lug those books about.

- Hi-Vis strips will help you be seen.

- Wipe-clean fabric helps keep you looking clean and will please Mum too.

- Rectangular shapes are good for files and folders.

- Expanding pockets will take bulky items like trainers.

- Side zipped pockets are great for carrying the extras like mobile phone, water and bus fares.

- An inside separate compartment for wet gear is handy and saves school book disasters.

- Finally prices vary from £10 to £90 but not always according to the quality.

First day

Everyone dreads walking into a room of strangers and the first day in a new class or school is daunting. So how can you make it easier to cope with? Well . . .

- Do your homework — find out beforehand as much as you can about the class or school and any children you already know.

- Don't go in with negative feelings like "I won't fit in" just go for it. You are as good as anyone else.

- Set yourself a goal to remember at least four names (by repeating them to yourself a few times) and make conversation with those people.

- Think of something to talk about before you go in the door, like "Do you have any pets?" or "What's your favourite sport?".

- Decide what you will tell people about yourself before you go in.

- Don't be late on your first day.

- Be properly dressed and go in with your head held high.

- Don't cling to one or two people but move around chatting to as many as you can.

Top tip

carry a hair bobble around in case you have a sports practice or you just want to tie it up. It's annoying having to look for one or borrow one from someone else. Put one in your pocket and keep it there.

The crumpled look

Just got up and school clothes still stuck in the bottom of your games bag? Don't turn up looking a crumpled mess. Hang all your clothes in the bathroom while you shower and close the door so that the bathroom gets all steamy. All the wrinkles in your clothes will miraculously disappear. Next time, make sure you roll your clothes in your bag to prevent those creases happening in the first place.

What's your name?

It's a real pain having to name all your possessions but an even bigger pain if stuff gets stolen and you have to tell your parents. Some things seem impossible to name and you can forget indelible pens and iron-on labels as these will not last the term. I find that laundry markers and sewn on labels are the best.

Hockey sticks — write your initials on the stick with a dark shade of nail varnish. Two coats and a top coat of clear varnish will see you though the year. (This works for the insides of football boots, cricket bats and tennis racquets too.)

Swimming goggles – loop an embroidered name tape around the stretchy headband and sew it firmly forming a circle. It won't come off or wash off.

A new best friend

If you get a new girl in the class (or you could be that new girl) how could you make yourself a new best friend? You really should get to know everyone, they might not be the same as you, but they might be just as much fun.

Everyone can be shy, but if you act confident you will start to believe that you really are and people will talk to you. If people are still hanging around with their original friends you should go and talk to them, instead of waiting around, they might just be shy too. Making new friends can be scary but remember that the others are just as nervous as you are. By positive, smile at people and that will put them at their ease and they'll be more likely to relax and open up to you in return.

When hanging round the school grounds watch your body language. Standing with a gang of friends with your arms crossed across your chest can look defensive and quite off-putting, if you fiddle with your hair that will make you seem nervous. When you meet a new girl or you are the new girl, make eye contact when someone is speaking to you to show that you are interested. Just make sure you are not staring at them.

I don't like Mondays

Monday morning's arrived and the school week stretches ahead. Re-boot yourself ready for the week ahead with these tips:

Get moving

It's a fact that exercise stimulates the feel good factors in your body and gets the blood pumping, which improves not only your body but your mood. Lazing around at break or on the sofa in the evening is tempting, but this will leave you feeling even more sluggish and fed up. Go on runs with your brothers, sisters or the dog and get fresh air. Exercise is so important and you'll feel much better.

Be happy

Smile at people during the day. If you smile at them, they'll smile back, just check it out, it works and gives you a good feeling!

Give back

This week why not give something to a good cause. There are lots of charities everywhere so there will be one local to you, it could be fun for you and your friends. You might not want to give money alone so maybe enter a fun run or something like that. Get all your friends to do it, get sponsored and dress up in funny clothes. Whatever you do, it will give you the feel better factor.

That's my goal

Try and set yourself a little task or goal – like stopping biting your nails or not leaving homework until the last minute, not big things but important little things that you really shouldn't do. If you stick to it you'll feel really pleased with yourself.

Lighten up

Lighten up by putting on your favourite CD or radio station on the way to school. You can't help but sing along and this lightens your mood and puts you in a good frame of mind to face the day ahead.

Start the day right

Don't skip breakfast no matter how rushed you are. Fill up on cereal, toast and fruit and set yourself up for the day ahead with that satisfied feeling. You could even eat your breakfast in the car or on the bus (but don't tell the driver!) It is too important to miss.

Feeling frazzled

If you are feeling stressed after the day at school and you have a long night of homework stretching ahead, then set aside ten minutes for a little bit of time on your own. Listen to your music or watch TV or even lie down for 10 minutes if that's what you like. This will enable you to prioritise and then set to work on the tasks ahead refreshed.

Dear Diary

Every night write down the positive things that have happened to you during the day, ignoring the negative. At the end of the week read it back and you'll be surprised how good you feel and you will have forgotten about all the bad things.

Brain drain

When summer arrives it's a good idea to have an extra bottle of water with you just in case you have an emergency hockey, netball or any other sports practice. Make sure you have packed a bottle of water for school and it doesn't have to be mineral water, good plain tap water, especially chilled, will do the job. Getting dehydrated at school can affect your mental performance and concentration. So drink more water and this will stop you feeling tired, irritable and distracted during the day — well this is what the studies show anyway!

Top tip

If you have pasta for dinner the night before set aside some plain cooked pasta to use for the next day's lunch box. Do not keep it for more than one day because this can cause tummy problems.

Bone up on calcium

When you are doing (or helping mum with) the early morning pack up, we all know about the five portions of fruit of veg a day, but did you know that a lot of kids don't get enough calcium in their diet? This is needed for strong bones and for kids aged 11-18 these are the following recommended three portions a day.

11-18 years (boy)   milk 250 ml   yogurt 200 g   cheese 45 g

11-18 years (girl)   milk 200 ml   yogurt 200 g   cheese 30 g

Dairy is one of the best sources so pop a tasty option in your daily packed lunch.

Packed lunches

Packed lunches are great if you have an activity over the lunch period as you can eat them quickly. But it can be nice to eat a hot meal every now and then.

Top tip

Bananas have roughly 100 calories and are easy to carry around. They give an instant pick- you-up. Eat them the same day or they will go black!

Simple snacks

By planning ahead here are a few meals to pop in the lunch box that can be made straight from the store cupboard and should easily fill the stomach as well as the lunch box.

Monday
Go for a nice bagel with your favourite filling, with a small piece of cake or a biscuit and a drink of juice or water.

Tuesday
Make up some home made pasta or rice salad the night before, adding your favorites such as tuna, sweetcorn, tomatoes, cucumber, peas or peppers. Put in an apple or few grapes.

Wednesday
Take a few pieces of chicken or ham as a change from a sandwich and eat this with some grapes and a packet of crisps.

Thursday
Ask Mum to make you a salad or make it yourself with some of your favourite ingredients like cherry tomatoes, hard-boiled egg or cooked beans or chick peas.

Friday
Top a tortilla with ham or turkey, add some salad and mayonnaise and wrap it in tin foil. Pop in some rice cakes and a Satsuma and a filling lunch will be waiting for you when you open the box.

Here are some recipe ideas:

Easy-peasy smoothie
Great for breakfast!

400g can of peaches in natural juice, drained
150g peach or apricot yoghurt
200ml orange juice
Tsp of honey
Blend everything until smooth – done!

Dead quick cookies (makes 24)
Something different for your lunch box that lasts all week.

150 g self-raising flour
150 g medium oatmeal
Pinch of salt
75 g caster sugar
75 g margarine
Milk to mix

1. Grease baking trays.
2. Heat oven 180C or gas mark 4.
3. Mix the dry ingredients and rub in margarine.
4. Add little milk to make stiff dough.
5. Roll out thin and cut into rounds.
6. Bake for about 15 minutes.

Chicken, Sweetcorn and Pasta Salad (serves 2)

A bit more of a challenge but worth the effort.

1 cooked chicken breast or smoked chicken, cut into bite-sized portions
115g pasta penne, cooked until al dente, then cooled
55g tinned or frozen sweetcorn
4 dried apricots, finely diced
2 spring onions, finely sliced
85g white cabbage, finely diced
25g sultanas or raisins
2 rashers of crispy bacon, crumbled

For the dressing:
2 tbsps good olive oil
2 tsps cider or white wine vinegar
1 tsp Dijon mustard
1 tsp liquid honey
Salt and ground black pepper

1. Combine all the dry ingredients, except the crispy bacon.
2. Whisk together the dressing ingredients and season to taste.
3. Toss the salad with the dressing, divide between the two lunchboxes and scatter with the crispy bacon.

Luxury Fruit Salad (serves 4)

85g dried coconut slices
1 mango, peeled and cut into bite-sized pieces
½ pineapple, peeled and cut into bite-sized pieces
115g water melon, peeled and cut into bite-sized pieces
½ honeydew melon peeled and cut into bite-sized pieces
2 passion fruits, pulp and seeds only
Juice and zest of 2 limes
2 tbsps caster sugar
150ml orange juice
2 tbsps chopped mint

Mix all the ingredients together and chill in the refrigerator
until ready to pop into plastic containers for your lunch,
for you and the whole family to share as a once-in-a-while
yummy treat.

On your bike

Cycling to school is cheap. Yes it's cheap and keeps you fit, but take some thought and care before you rush out of the door. Here are my top ten tips to keep you safe.

1. We all need our brains, even if our parents don't think we use them enough! So protect yours with a helmet. You will soon get used to the fact that no-one has yet invented one that looks cool or even remotely attractive but get over it!

2. Get the helmet fitted properly and always fasten up the straps.

3. Make sure your bike is the right size for you. Adjust it so that you can stand with your feet flat on the floor when straddling the top bar.

4. Check your brakes, oil and chain.

5. Check your tyres and pressure.

6. Wear high vis clothing – jacket, shoe laces, back pack.

7. Never wear headphones whilst cycling – you need to concentrate and hear what's around you.

8. Stick to cycle lanes and watch for car doors opening.

9. Watch out for wet leaves on your route.

10. Keep your chrome bright by removing rusty bits with scrunched up tin foil – it won't keep you any safer but at least you will look good.

Top tip

If you wear mascara for school make sure you wear waterproof mascara in case it starts raining, you start crying or you forget that you have swimming – black streaks are a dead give away!

Be seen

I'm sure that everyone has heard of high visibility jackets and a lot of people don't want to wear them, but have you heard of other high visibility clothes? You can get lots of different high-vis clothes. You can get hats, scarves and even shoe laces. Also available are strips that you can stick on bags and you can get swimming style bags that are easy to carry around. All these items are available in a selection of different colours in many shops.

Hotel freebies

When away in a hotel, we've all spotted the freebies in the bathroom and these can come in very handy in the school bag or on a school holiday.

1. The little mini sewing kits make a handy lightweight kit to stow in the bathroom cupboard — with a needle and cotton or spare button for emergency repairs.

2. They also hold safety pins, which can be very handy if you bust a skirt button at an embarrassing moment.

3. The shower caps are great for keeping your hair dry and come in their own little packaging — so are easy to take with you.

4. The mini vanity kits are also great when you need a cotton bud or a mini nail file when away from home.

5. Individual shower gels, shampoos and conditioners are also great for school trips or camping holidays or an overnight stay at friends.

6. These also keep your luggage weight down if you have to carry it or pay excess baggage.

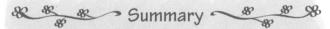

Summary

Right, that's got you up and fed and out the door so let's move on to where the trouble or fun starts — SCHOOL!

chapter 2
P.S.H.E

What's a mushroom?
The place where they store the school dinners!

What is it all about?

Most parents don't have a clue what this stands for or what's included in these lessons. P.S.H.E. stands for **Personal, Social and Health Education**. Basically all the stuff we need to know but parents don't want to talk about. It covers topics such as:

- Drugs
- Hygiene
- Bullying (see chapter 6, page 99)
- Relationships
- Healthy eating
- Health issues
- Fitness

All of this aims to help us kids understand how we are developing personally and socially and tackles moral and cultural issues. It takes in parts of the curriculum and goes beyond it into assemblies, project work plus clubs and out of school activities. A good teacher will help children build up their confidence, take responsibility and get the most out of life.

Mates for life

It's always good to be friends with people in your class not enemies because you're probably going to be in a class with them for the next 5 years. Here are some tips:

1. Everyone makes mistakes and friends don't always do exactly what you want them to, but do try not to tell them "I told you so" because it will just upset them. "Shutting up" is all about listening to what is going on in their life, even when yours is going smoothly. They will think you are a great friend if you just listen to them for a bit.

2. Always tell your friends the truth; it might be hard but it's easier then having them being embarrassed later on.

3. There is a difference between telling someone the truth and being horrible so try and say things in a nice way.

4. Your friends aren't going to be perfect, no-one is, but never get embarrassed by what they are doing because that's who they are. You wouldn't want them not to be free to be themselves around you.

5. If you are planning on doing nothing one Sunday and just lounging around watching TV, but your friend wants to do something different with you, you should. Maybe it's the last chance for a while for just the two of you to be together. Your friend will be really pleased you chose them over repeats of The X Factor.

6. When you get a new best friend those first few weeks of friendship are probably the best. It's normal for friendships to calm down after a while. If this happens it doesn't give you an excuse to stop making an effort. You should make sure you stay in touch by sending the odd text just to say hi. Make sure you tell her how great she looks in an outfit, even if she's worn it 100 times before or send her a little card if she's feeling ill.

7. If your friends tell you their secrets never tell anyone else. Your friends will have told you them in confidence. I don't think they would really appreciate it if secrets got twisted and spread around the whole class.

Winners and losers

When you get into an argument with your friends you need to listen to their side of the story. Your friends won't mind if you admit you're wrong they should respect you for it. If it is the other way round though and you're right, just forget about it, don't rub it in and try to continue as normal. A good friend knows when to back down.

Top tip
Remember - all medicines are drugs but not all drugs are medicines.

How to win an argument

However tempting it might be to shout in an argument, don't. People will listen more if you reply in a calm way.

Eating disorder information

During school life we will all sadly see someone with an eating disorder. An eating disorder is an illness that almost always starts from some kind of emotional distress and results in obsessive, unhealthy relationships with food. It can cause a person to diet or comfort-eat. Also, dealing with difficult changes, or catty comments about their weight, can trigger someone to develop an unhealthy attitude to food. In a big school there will be sufferers and here is some help for you to understand the main types of eating disorders.

Anorexia
Sufferers have a distorted view of their own body shape and weight thinking that they're fat even when they are very thin and leading them to starve themselves deliberately.

Bulimia
This is a cycle of stuffing yourself with food to the point where you are sick, or binge eating and then forcing yourself to vomit before your body can digest anything.

Compulsive or Comfort Eating

This involves binge eating to help control emotions.

You can try to help someone with an eating disorder if you spot it, but many sufferers try to hide their condition. But here are some signs that you may notice:

1. Skipping meals.

2. Always looking at the calorie content.

3. Only eating very low calorie foods.

4. Sudden loss of weight.

5. Sudden gain in weight.

6. Behaving defensively when asked about how much food they eat.

7. Wearing loose fitting clothes to disguise their body shape.

8. Rushing away from the table straight after meals. This could be to make themselves sick.

If you suspect a friend has eating problems you need to take a gentle approach and here are a few tips:

1. Set a time and place to talk so your conversation won't be overheard.

2. Voice your concerns but be caring and gentle.

3. Encourage friends to talk but don't lecture them. Listen to your friend's reactions and do not be judgmental.

4. Don't ever try to force them to talk about it, just let them know that you're concerned and supporting them.

5. Be patient, demanding to know everything or offering simple solutions such as "Why don't you just eat something and then you'll be okay" will not be helpful.

6. Make sure your friend is told about their good points and their great personality rather than their appearance. You want him or her to feel confident about themselves.

7. And don't avoid the subject. Talk openly about your worries because if you avoid the issue they most probably will too. Try to get to the point, in a caring way though.

A sucker for juice

Drinking fizzy drinks can rot your teeth, but not just fizzy drinks. Pure orange juice has a lot of acid in it. An easy solution would be not to drink any of these but that's not going to happen. We all love them so try drinking them through a straw. This way you can still enjoy it but it bypasses your teeth.

Knitter not picker

Picking at snacks all evening is not good for you and is usually just something to do with your hands. You won't eat if you are busy. Learn to knit and keep your hands and mind occupied. You are in good company as many of the stars knit while sitting on the film sets, like Julia Roberts!

Kill the germs

Did you know that most of the germs in a school are spread by people not washing their hands? You may say that you do wash your hands but a quick dip under a cold tap isn't enough. I know school toilets aren't the nicest of all loos but I'm sure that they have sinks and a bit of soap. So give hands a thorough wash using soap under the hot tap. Use the soap and get in between your fingers, your nails and the palms of your hands. This doesn't take long, so instead of rushing take it slow and wash well. If your school really doesn't have any soap or even hot water, get some antibacterial gel, keep it in your pocket and this kills all germs. NB: It's worth a complaint too to the school if soap and water really are absent!

Hidden germs

Always wash your hands before eating, it may be common sense but many people don't. It may be good manners to put your hand in front of your mouth when coughing or sneezing but the germs stay there to pass around. Also did you know that computer keyboards carry thousands of germs? When you touch it you pick up those germs. Antibacterial wipes should be used to clean keyboards regularly.

The sniff test

There is nothing worse than sitting next to the stinker. With all the information we are given at school and bombarded with on TV, there is really no excuse to go around smelly, but there's always one. It could come from B.O., the feet or somewhere in between! It's almost as bad when they try to cover up one bad smell with another and the result makes you gag! No amount of the latest designer fragrance will mask the disgusting whiff after a games lesson or rugby game — so don't try it. Dive in the shower, scrub and spray. But seriously, how do you tell someone? It's not easy — especially if they are a friend and feelings can be hurt.

Route A, the direct one, can be the best way if done in a light-hearted fashion. Try:

"Hey, have you been doing games today, because you kind of pong a bit."

Top tip

Don't ever put ordinary soap on your face. There are plenty of face washes and other cleansers and using those with a hot flannel will help keep your skin clean and spot free.

More discreet ways to get the message across are:

"I have found this really good deodorant/body spray, everyone says it works great, have you tried it?"

"It's a good idea to use a matching shower gel and deodorant so you don't mix smells, shall I get you some for your birthday/Xmas?"

"It's funny how clothes pick up smells that linger, have you noticed that when you put your clothes back on?"

Stick 'em up

If you are ever at school and your hem comes down, it can be really annoying. This probably will happen to you, so instead of letting it bother you, try using clear sticky tape to stick it back up – on the inside (of course) then no-one will see or know about it. It works for trousers as well as skirts.

Scent of success

Don't cover up nasty body odour with body sprays and perfume. But what's just as bad is stale perfume. Perfume can go stale when left out of its box in daylight. Keep all sprays or perfumes in their boxes in a cool, dry place and safely off sunny window sills. They can explode in direct sun.

Trainer treat

Pinch dry, used tea bags and those silicone sachets Mum finds in her new shoes or handbags and put them in your trainers. This is a great cheap way to make your shoes smell better but remember to remove them before wearing!

Sweet smelling hair

Hair picks up smells from around and about quite easily. Smells that you just don't want in your hair. Things like bonfire smoke, cooking smells or the sweaty school smell. So keep you hair clean by washing it at least once every two days. You can buy shampoos and conditioners for all types of hair. Maybe your hair gets greasy so buy a special non-greasy shampoo. Try to match your hair products so they're all the same. Shampoo does not have to be expensive (but it can be) so use it properly. Wash well but rinse, rinse, rinse is the answer to shiny hair. Keep your brushes clean too. You can do this by taking out the hair and washing them in the shower with you. Don't brush the smells back in, so do this every week.

Dry shampoo

In the 1980s, most girls owned 'dry shampoo'. It's a powder that you put on hair and then blow dry it after. Suddenly dry shampoo is making a come back and can be an essential for saving time on a school day. Check out the shops and give it a try.

Better breath

Food pieces stuck in your braces not only look awful but are guaranteed to see even your best friends running away in horror, even worse they can also cause bad breath. You cannot even chew gum to help. So cut up food into really small pieces and carry a small mirror to check that the tell-tale lettuce leaf has not lodged itself into your front teeth. Carry a toothbrush and use it after lunch at school. You will have to avoid fizzy drinks and toffees while the braces are on, so stick to this after they come off to kick start a much healthier lifestyle.

Wash basket case

If in doubt stick it in the wash. If clothes really do whiff then wash them! This doesn't mean, however, trying on a top and aiming it for the wash bag instead of hanging it back up. Yes we've all done it! But seriously, clothes, particularly school uniforms, pick up smells and muck, so blouses and undies need changing daily — that's a definite. For the skirts and blazers these can be hung up by an open window to refresh them and checked for washing at the weekend.

De-fuzz

Take it from me, I speak from experience! Don't try to handle a razor without help! Shaving your legs for the first time can leave you with more trouble than stubble. It's all too easy to cut yourself when it's steamy and slippy in the shower and you have a dangerous implement in hand. Better still do it in the bath and go carefully, a blood bath in the shower is scary and tell-tale scars round the ankle are not a good look!

Sleep tight

Once in a while re-charge the batteries with an early night. None of us ever admits to being tired, but a nice warm bath, cup of hot chocolate and a duvet can work wonders for the temper. Let the homework wait until tomorrow, tape what's on TV and curl up for 12 hours of therapy.

Tidy your room

We have all heard that one, but seriously a tidy space can mean you work better. So plan, chuck out, clean and organise once in a while. Plan the space on a piece of paper if it makes it easier for you.

- Clothes — pass on or chuck clothes that don't fit or are gritty.

- Toys and games (missing bits or broken) — bin them.
- Not your stuff — give it back.
- Books — read or donate to someone.
- Food or crockery under the bed — get Mum involved and get rid.
- Clean up what's left.
- Wash dirty bedding, curtains, and cushions.
- Shake rugs.
- Vacuum inside wardrobe or cupboards as they are fluff magnets.
- Have separate areas for study, sleep and slobbing out.
- For dressing, stash clothes in cupboards and drawers and get a big wash basket for the dirty stuff.
- Use see-through boxes for make-up, school supplies, jewellery and stack them.
- Stick all pens etc in a mug.
- Stick photos on the walls or doors or clip on a line of string.
- Get a good reading light near the bed.
- A desk or table is a must if you do your homework in here.

Now relax and enjoy your space and be honest — it's much better this way isn't it? ;)

Summer sport

To stay extra fresh at school in summer why not take an extra pair of pants or socks with you and you're ready for a quick change if things get sticky.

Mirror motivation

Help get motivated to lose weight or tone up through exercise, by taking a photo of you from behind. You'll be amazed what knowing what you really look like to others will do to spur you on and it may also help you decide if that micro-mini really does suit you!

Be cold sore smart

Cold sores have a nasty way of sneaking up on you when you have no ointment in the house and it's the school disco the next day. Freeze a wet peppermint tea bag and press it on the tingle. This will help keep it at bay overnight until you can make a dash to the chemist.

Eye workout

Doing homework in front of a screen can strain your eyes and make them feel tired and gritty.
Try this to refresh them while your computer takes a break:

Look straight ahead for 3 minutes at an object about 5 metres away. Close your eyes for about 30 seconds your eyes will relax but it's no substitute for a proper rest from the screen so turn it off and do something else, an hour at a time on computer is more than enough.

Hug don't hunch

Sitting hunched over the computer is no good for your muscles. If you can't drag yourself away outside for a quick kick about or offer to wash the dishes, try this at the desk. Hug yourself tight, stretching your arms across your chest and trying to reach as far as you can. Hold and repeat.

Leg lesson

Ankles suffer too from long-term computer usage. Rotate them clockwise then anti-clockwise 6 times each and wiggle your toes for a count of 10.

Brace yourself

Around the age of 12 to 14 many of you will be looking up the dentist's nose to be told that you need braces! When your parents have picked themselves up off the floor from the shock of the waiting list or price, they are worth considering. A year or two's pain will mean a life of gain so ask your Mum "What price can she put on a nice smile?"

Seriously, nowadays only the most serious cases will be considered by the NHS and the rest are likely to cost Mum and Dad around £2,000, so bear this in mind when you are asking them for that very expensive laptop for Christmas.

Once you have made the leap and had them fitted the rest is up to you. You will need to get up a few minutes earlier each morning to allow time for cleaning. Getting used to them will take a few weeks and the first week is the worst.

Sore cheeks are agony because the wires cut into them and many suffer a year of cracked lips. But they are there until the dentist decides to take them off and complaining will make no difference. Why is it they are so unsympathetic to a whining teenager?

So how can you help yourself? Well cleaning is the key. Cleaning the teeth is not as easy as it was. Little brushes may be needed to get into the difficult spaces. Failing to clean after eating will result in puffy bleeding gums and tooth decay. So carry a travel brush wherever you go. After the braces come off, no matter how careful you have been the teeth will still be stained and may require professional scaling and polishing. For over a year you will need time off school to attend appointments but never miss one as gaps in the dentist's appointment book are much rarer than the ones in your teeth!

Head lice lingo

We've all heard about head lice, sometimes called nits. Head lice are itchy. They won't clear up on their own and have to be treated and this can be embarrassing all around. Girls are more likely to get head lice than boys. You can be any age. It is not a sign of dirty hair as they are happy living in clean hair too. Check your hair and kids with them should stay off school until clear. You can comb them out, it's really easy.

Try coating your hair with a thick layer of conditioner and then comb it through section by section until all the head lice are out. You can buy lots of different shampoos and lotions but whichever treatment is used, a follow-up check using a nit comb must be carried out a few days after the first course of treatment. The best way to prevent head lice is to regularly check the scalps of your whole family and treat them as soon as any live lice are found.

Well armed

There is a new vaccination for girls aged 12 to 13 called the HPV vaccine. All schoolgirls will have the option to have it, but you don't have to if your family doesn't want you to. There is a website to tell you lots about it, the address is **www.immunisation.nhs.uk/Vaccines/HPV**. You will be well informed before having it by your teacher in P.S.H.E., or by the school nurse.

By having the vaccination, it will reduce your risk of getting cervical cancer by over 70%. You will get three injections over a few months for full protection. The nurse will give you the vaccination in your upper arm. If your parents don't want you to have it then that's fine, your school, teachers or nurse won't make you have it but they will want to talk to your parents. Parents have to sign and return a consent form before the vaccination is due.

First aid

Research shows that children lack first aid skills. I have gathered all this information from the British Red Cross website which is in the back of my book. Obviously an adult's help is best but, if you are on your own, these procedures will help . . .

Treating burns and scalds

1. Cool the burn as quickly as possible by placing the affected area under cold water for at least 10 minutes.

2. Raise the limb to reduce swelling.

3. Cover the injury using a clean pad or kitchen film, and seek medical advice. Dial 999 in serious cases.

Treating sprains and strains

A common experience on the school field. Immediate help is really simple just:

1. Raise the injured part.

2. Ice — apply ice or a cold pad to the injured area.

3. Compress the injury using a bandage or soft padding.

Nosebleeds

Not normally dangerous but very annoying.

1. Ensure the person is sitting down. Advise them to tilt their head forward to allow the blood to drain from the nostrils.

2. Ask the person to pinch the end of their nose hard and continue to breathe through their mouth.

3. After 10 minutes, release the pressure. If the bleeding has not stopped, reapply the pressure for up to two further periods of 10 minutes.

4. If bleeding continues, seek medical advice.

Severe bleeding

Your main aim is to stem the flow of blood. If you have disposable gloves available, use them. It is important to reduce the risk of cross infection.

1. Check if there is an object stuck in the wound.

2. If there is nothing there, press on the wound with your hand, ideally over a clean pad, & secure with a bandage.

3. If the wound is on an arm or leg raise the injured limb above the level of the heart.

How to call 999

999 is only for an immediate response where a crime is happening or someone is in immediate danger. If you do have to call the emergency services do it carefully like this:

• Remember that you will be talking to a call centre which could be miles away.

• Speak clearly. Give your name and location / address.

• If it is an incident outside, like a car crash, they will want to know where it is, so try to get the name of the road, the road number (like the A1079) or name of the village.

• If you're at home you may have to follow instructions while they get to you, so stay calm but never put yourself in danger.

• Try to get help from an adult.

Home alone

There will be a time when we all have to stay in by ourselves, either before or after school or on a weekend and here are some quick tips to help you be safe and sound when you are home alone:

* Make sure you can lock and unlock all doors and windows. Lock yourself in the house as you may not hear someone come in if you are upstairs.

* If you are going to operate any appliances make sure you are shown how to do them properly.

* Know where the first aid kit is and learn how to stop bleeding from a cut and how to deal with a little burn.

* Know where the torch is just in case there is a power cut, but never ever light candles.

* Pin up a list of phone numbers for Mum, Dad, neighbours, work etc. and make sure you know how to call 999. You could put them in your mobile or memorise your parent's numbers.

* Ask Mum or Dad to leave a spare set of keys in the house in case you lose yours.

* Don't put your name and address on your door key, if you lose it you will make it very easy for a burglar to break into your home.

- If you must cook some food, use the microwave, they don't have open flames and shut off automatically and this is a lot safer than using the oven.

- A word of warning on microwaves. Hot steam can escape and burn you so always use oven mitts or a tea towel to open anything you've warmed up from the microwave and keep the dish well away from your face

- If all this sounds just too dangerous and strikes fear into you perhaps the best thing when you go home from school is just lie on the settee and watch TV until Mum or Dad gets in.

Good manners

BURRRP!

Good table manners are essential later in life, so you may as well start as you mean to go on. Burping at the table may well be good manners in China but it's not where I live. You don't have to put on a tuxedo for dinner (although experiencing a nice posh meal once in a while can be fun) but try at least to put some clothes on at the table and not sit there in your underwear.

Eating chips with your fingers may be OK at the seaside but make sure the proper cutlery is used at home and at friends' houses or you may not get that second invite. Napkins can be good to save your best dress or trousers for stains just before you go out and how many times do parents complain about our habits, only to be told how wonderfully helpful we were at friends' houses. Help with the dishes at home once in a while just to shock them!

It goes a long way

Simply saying "please" and "thank you" at all times is likely to keep you in everyone's good books so don't forget it. When you are thanked say "you're welcome" and it will go down even better. If you can manage it, try being good mannered even when you lose a game, by not sulking or taking your ball home!

Pimple prevention

Everyone gets spots. There are lots of treatments for them but most are unnecessary. Baking powder and water is a great way to get rid of dead skin and spots, you just simply rub it over your face then wash off. Some people apply toothpaste to the spot and leave it to dry, and then wash it off. It's that easy.

Teacher: "This is the third time I've had to tell you off this week, what have you got to say about that?"

Pupil: "Thank Heavens it's Friday!"

School day myths and misconceptions

Granny might tell you otherwise but here is the truth about a few girlie problems.

1. **If you cut your hair it will grow back even stronger and quicker.**

   Sadly this is not true. Cutting your hair will only make it shorter and it will still grow back at exactly the same speed as before. Hair grows about 1.25 cm (.5 in) a month; cutting off the split ends will make it look healthier and thicker but it won't grow back any longer.

2. **Wearing make-up gives you spots.**

   It is not a good look to go to school covered in thick make-up every day and some of the adult brands can be harsh on our young skins, but if you use gentle formulas and the brands that suit you, the make-up itself will not cause the spots; the causes of zits are not cleansing thoroughly or simply just going through puberty. If you don't take your make-up off, then you will get spots.

3. **You mustn't wash your hair during a period.**

   This is disgusting; do you really want to go without washing your hair for days on end? I don't think you would. There is absolutely no truth in this rumour — in fact you could sweat even more and find that your hair gets even worse during your period and it's even more important to shower every day and wash your hair to keep it clean and fresh.

4. Everyone at school will know when a girl is on her period.

This is certainly not true. No-one could possibly know unless you tell them. You may have tell-tale signs like spots or a slight bloating feeling in the tummy or a mood swing, but these can happen for all sorts of reasons at any time of the month. However, it is a weird fact that girls who go around together a lot of the time in a group, sometimes end up having their periods all at the same time as each other, so don't be surprised if that happens to you. Just pity the poor teacher who has to face a class full of hormonal girls.

5. Periods mainly last for a week.

Not really, no two people are the same. Most periods will last for an average of 4-5 days but it could even mean anything from 3-8 days. Not everyone has a straight 28-day cycle either, some are slightly longer and some are slightly shorter especially in the early days.

6. Chocolate and chips bring you out in spots.

Overdoing sugar and fried junk food is never a good idea but the fact is that these particular foods have never been proven to cause acne. Some people might get a break-out after eating a lot of chocolate while others are perfectly fine with it. It is what works for you. Check out your skin, if it flares up at certain times then it could help to cut back on a particular food type, but it is a case of sucking it to see what makes the difference for you.

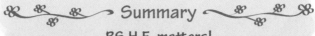

Summary

P.S.H.E. matters!

P.S.H.E. is not like a normal lesson. It should be a place where you feel comfortable speaking to the boys and girls in your class about all sorts of stuff like:

1. Being a good person.

2. Talking about topical issues.

3. Recognising choices that you can make.

4. Agreeing with others to follow rules for the good of you all.

5. Understanding what improves and harms the environment.

6. Contributing in your own little way to the life of the class and whole school.

7. You'll talk about growing up, parts of your body and about medicines and household products which can be harmful if not used properly.

8. You should learn a bit about how to respect other people and you might learn about different beliefs, but you learn more about that in religious education.

At the end of school you will have gained something from this to make you ready for working life.

chapter 3

Learn your lesson

What is an angler?
Someone who is very good at maths!

Tutors help

You're not going to be the best in every subject and there is going to be at least one subject you will struggle with. Well don't. It really does help if you have a  good teacher but if you don't like your teacher or don't get their style of teaching then you should have a look around for a tutor. He or she can give you 'one to one' help in their specialised subject to get you over a problem or to help you pass the exam. It's normally for an hour a week or can be good for the odd half day session or week's crammer before an exam. There are lots of tutors and many advertise in the local paper. So there will be one near you and it may be the one thing you want to keep private until you get your confidence back.

CVs

It is never too early to start your CV! This is short for the Latin curriculum vitae (loosely meaning 'course of life') and gives details of your personal and educational qualifications. CVs have lots of different things on them. You put on your grades from exams and music lessons, your hobbies and interests and maybe what sports teams you played for. You need a CV for getting any job at any age. The presentation of yours should be clear and neat — remember first impressions matter. They should be about a page long but as you get older you may write three pages, but never send more than that. Don't go over the top, use bullet points and bold text and make it eye-catching.

Always make sure that the spelling is correct before sending it in. Put the most recent grades first and get to the point, don't babble on about other stuff. Start a CV now while you are younger to remember what you have achieved and it will feel easier when the time comes for the real thing.

The confidence trick

Exams are a huge part of school there are exams around every corner. They are a big part of your life too, they help you get a place at college, and they also help you to get a job. They're never going to go away so don't ignore them, just prepare yourself as best you can. Everyone feels stressed and panics right up to seeing the paper. Help yourself by being as confident as possible. Cut down the worries by:

- Having everything you need and then a spare: pencils, pens, cartridges, rubber, ruler and calculator (possibly).

- Have a good energy meal beforehand, i.e. a banana.

- Drink water before and try to go to the toilet.

- Make sure you arrive 5 minutes early.

- Dress comfortably and in layers. You can always take a jumper off but you can't put a layer on if you are cold.

- Take some tissues (for obvious reasons).

- Look confident; don't hang about in the doorway looking nervous. Walk into the room with your head up. Look the part and you will succeed.

- There are some exam tips to come later in the book.

Get ahead of the game

From infant school onwards we've all been tested in spelling,
tables, SATs and exams and our parents get the results. To
avoid the grade card shocks get your parents to help you
pass with the exam-time survival tips below:

1. When you've had a bit of time off school you should have
   one of your friends write down what you've missed and
   bring your books to your house for you to catch up on.
   Make sure you understand and be sure to ask the
   teacher when you get back if you don't. If you've missed
   it you can't revise it.

2. You never actually realise how long revision will take
   you to do. You should start revising about 4 weeks in
   advance. This way it's not all crammed in the night
   before your exam.

3. It's true that children in Years 6 to 8 can only concentrate for 20 minutes at a time. So short breaks, fresh air and a drink every now and then can refresh you, your concentration will be much better too.

4. Start with your weaker subjects, and then you can get them out of the way. Then you have your favourite and probably stronger subjects left. So then you don't have to worry.

5. Make sure to keep doing your regular sports and/or musical activities, as it is good to have your brain working on different subjects.

6. Revise in a room that is quiet with a desk with no distractions, you will get way more done.

7. When it's your school exam week, try not to plan any major events with friends or family as you'll need all the time you have to revise.

8. Make sure you actually understand what you are learning. Ensure what you have copied into your book makes sense and is correct otherwise all your revision would be for nothing.

9. Let your parents test you on what you've learnt so far.

10. Your parents will try to help you and honestly it is a good idea to let them; you never know they might have a few helpful ideas.

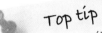

Top tip

Always go to the toilet before you start, whether you think you want to or not. You need all the time you can get in the exam so you don't want to be leaving the room to go to the toilet.

Getting better marks

Exams are timed tests and allow you to show how much you know and what you understand. Everyone has them in their school life. But think positive — examiners want to give you good marks if you can simply show them that you understand the subjects that you've been studying. Some people find exams extremely stressful but some others just sail through them.

Repetition

Only make your point once, you don't get any extra marks for repeating yourself over and over again. Phrasing it differently doesn't help you either, they will just ignore it. Examiners see this a lot and say it's just a time waster.

Stressed out!

At times of worry:

1. Take mini breaks through the day to breathe deeply.

2. Exercise — doing lots of activities provides relief from stress or even a brisk walk will do it.

3. Pace yourself — school isn't a race.

4. Write stuff to do on a list and tick it off during the day.

5. Sleep 8 to 10 hours a night.

6. Use a planner and have time for revision, sleep, eating and friendships.

7. Be positive. If you say you can do it then you probably will.

8. Talking to friends can reduce your stress.

9. Be calm before you start the day.

10. Stay healthy. Eat healthily when under pressure and your brain will work better.

Check it out

Always know where and when the exam is. If it is in a room you've not been in before, go and check it out before so that there's no last minute panic or surprises when you can't find the room. If you don't know when the exam is, I don't think this would happen but just in case, you should ring someone who is taking the exam too. Always get there about 10-15 minutes before it starts if you can, so you can sit down and be prepared.

Top tip

Before any exam, make sure that there are no notes or crib sheets accidentally left in your pocket or pencil case. If you are caught with a scribbled note, even if you didn't purposely mean to cheat you can have your exams cancelled and that's all the work down the drain. I don't think you'd want this.

Speak out

If you feel sick during an exam, make sure you tell the teacher. You won't get penalised if you have a real reason and you don't do so well.

Never fear

Just try to think of the exam as any other normal school day and follow your normal routine as far as you possibly can to help you relax. And take a watch in with you, but make sure that any alarms are disabled. Make sure any mobile phones are turned off; if it went off in the exam you'd be in big trouble.

Bits and bobs

Get together all your pens, pencils, rubbers, rulers, calculators and whatever you need well in advance of the exam. If you don't have everything you need, you will have to go out and buy the missing stuff.

Keep calm

Try and avoid stressful situations on the exam day. Don't have a row with your parents or siblings and also be sure to leave plenty of time to get to your exam, there might be really bad traffic and you don't want to be late. If you are on the bus, go early. If it helps take something for luck like a lucky charm or teddy.

Snap, crackle, pop

Once you're in the exam room make sure you've opened water bottle tops, unwrapped cough sweets etc. before you start. The examiner won't really like it if you are making a noise during the exam, I don't think that other people sitting the exam will either.

Wobbly bits

Make sure you've not got a wobbly desk or chair. If you desk does wobble wedge a piece of paper underneath it or this could be very annoying when you start writing. If it's really bothering you, tell the teacher and they will happily get you a new one.

A.R.T.Q.

This is a tip from my old Headteacher, Mr Bryan. Always Read The Question. If you don't understand it read it through again until you do. Once you are given the signal to start, read the exam paper carefully. When you do tackle the questions, most students will attempt their strongest area first and leave the weakest until last. There is no right or wrong way, just decide to start with whichever suits you best. It can be quite scary when you look round and everyone's started writing immediately. Try to ignore what everyone else is doing; what they're doing is not important to you. Allow as much time as you need for preparation before you get stuck in. People have different ways of doing things; just make sure you understand what you are reading. Time spent planning answers is not wasted time, it can be of great benefit.

End in sight

If you are running out of time when you get to the last question, you can just write brief notes about what you know, but try to make it make sense because the examiner hasn't got a crystal ball and can't guess what you might know. Try not to leave any questions out unless you have no clue what it's about. You should try to write something, you might get a mark, you might not, but you're not going to get a mark if you don't write anything.

Don't panic

Try to relax during your exam. If you *do go* blank or start to panic, put your pen down and breathe steadily. Close your eyes and count to 50 and you will find that in 1 or 2 minutes your brain will become clear and you will be able to focus on the job in hand again. Every now and again, stretch for a minute, stretch your neck and your hands and this will help you relax and will prevent cramp.

Time's up

Just before the end, don't be afraid to make corrections and additions to your answers. Stay in control and make sure anything you want to add is clearly marked so the examiner knows where they should really be looking in your work. Make sure that your writing is legible. Don't leave the exam room early. Even if you *do* finish before the time is up, another important point may come to you and further crucial marks can be gained. Check your answers if you have time. If you have lots of time, add to your answers and check again.

They think it's all over

After the exam unwind by talking to friends and share your feelings and thoughts with them as this helps reduce stress. Once you've released all your worries and stresses you will be fine and what you did won't really bother you any more until the results come in!

Team players

I'm sure there have been lots of times when
you have been sat at home staring at the wall
thinking about the scary prospect of the exams
ahead of you. Don't worry, everyone has or will do
at one point. Think about the power of teamwork.
Ask your siblings or friends or parents to help
you revise. Sometimes two heads can be better than one.

Remember, remember!

How many times have you tried to recall a date in history
or how many days there are in a month and relied upon a
little saying to help you? Memory aids can be a useful way of
earning extra points in an exam, impressing your friends or
winning that quiz. Here are some examples:-

* The fate of the six wives of Henry V111 was varied and
  bloody in this order: "divorced, beheaded, died, divorced,
  beheaded, survived". Now all you have to remember are
  their names! Err. . .?

* We all learn that it's generally "i" before "e" except after
  "c" but this rhyme will help you sort out the trickier
  nouns from the verbs as follows: "S is the verb and C
  is the noun, that's the rule that runs the town". Now you
  should be able to get "practise and practice" right, as
  well as "license and licence". "The vet has a licence and
  practises his skills at his practice in town". Get it?

* Where's Sicily on the map? "Long legged Italy's kicking
  Sicily right into the middle of the Mediterranean sea."

- Stalactites or stalagmites? Well the "tights" come down of course — from the ceiling. Which means the 'mites' run up from the floor.

- Do our clocks go back or forward in spring? As the saying goes it's "spring forward, fall back" and all you need to know now is that the fall is autumn in the USA.

- Put hard-to-remember poems, lines from a play or French verbs to music for a great aid to learning. You can remember the words to your favourite pop songs for decades as you will know from having to listen to Mum and Dad singing away to 'oldies' in the car! And didn't we all sing the alphabet and remember it from about age 3? No musical ability required.

- Some words are downright impossible to spell and this one comes up tops in any poll.

  DIARRHOEA — "**D**ash **I**n **A** **R**eal **R**ush **H**urry **O**r **E**lse **A**ccident" should do the trick.

- "Richard Of York Gave Battle In Vain" is the old saying that helps us remember the colours of the rainbow. But you could update it with your own saying so long as it's memorable.

- Maria in The Sound of Music taught the children the musical notes in the song "DO-RE-MI" and we learn the notes on the lines of the treble clef E, G, B, D, F by "**Every Good Boy Deserves Football**" and the spaces spell out "**FACE**".

- Even doctors have a sense of humour and often use their own abbreviations to note symptoms on patients' files with "TATT" being "Tired All The Time". More seriously lives can be saved with the use of similar acronyms:

ABC – **A**irways, **B**reathing, **C**irculation, is what to check when dealing with a casualty.

FIRE – **F**ind the fire, **I**nform people, **R**estrict the spread, **E**vacuate the area.

Ask, ask and ask again

If you are in class and you don't understand something, this is completely normal and expected; nobody knows everything or always grasps it straight away. It could be that the teacher hasn't explained it very well. Ask the teacher clearly and politely as that is what they are there for. Some people feel really dumb asking questions but what's really dumb is not asking questions – it's the only way you learn.

So, you put up your hand and ask the teacher and hopefully they will explain it – end of story. But still you don't follow. No, you are not being thick and you must not leave it there. Try asking once more and listen to the reply. Still not sunk in? Then ask the teacher to spare you a few minutes at break or maybe they will suggest this, to go over it again. This means you don't disturb others in the class and take up their time as you would hate it if they did it to you. So don't worry at all, I bet you're not the only one who doesn't get it.

What are they for?

Teachers are teachers because they are clever (in one subject at least), they are there to teach you, so don't be naughty or give them cheek because you are the one that will be in trouble. They are just doing their job. They're nice people really so trust them. Remember they have kids too so they know all the tricks in the book.

Dream roles

Most British children dream of fame and fortune, 1 in 4 children want to become celebrities when they grow up, that's according to new figures.

25% of children in Wales want to be footballers, 26% of children in the North East want to be teachers, and 24% of children in the East Midlands want to be vets.

Is this true and where do you fit in?

Help at hand

If you're stuck always ask your teacher. The internet isn't always reliable. The same goes for homework. Don't just copy and paste it from the Internet. Use it, but put it in your own words, at least you will understand it better and in any case the teachers will know straight away if you pinched it.

Homework block

Most teachers say that you should do your homework in a comfortable quiet place with no distractions but trying to do your homework with no distractions is really tricky. Some people prefer to work when there is a bit of music in the background. If you are having trouble getting a bit of peace for homework, don't panic – talk to your parents first and they will probably set a time for you to do it with no one else around. At some schools they might have homework clubs during or after school where pupils can go and study.

Fridays off

Treat yourself to Friday evenings off. Many schools don't give weekend homework preferring you to get some fresh air, play and relax. If you do need to catch up on any missed work squeeze it in over the weekend but relax too.

Make a note

When you get home you will often have forgotten what you were supposed to be doing for homework. At the time it's given, write down the instructions clearly in a separate homework diary. These instructions should include when the homework will be collected, it may not be the next day and therefore there is some leeway as to when it can be done. But! Avoid bunching, which means you could end up with four lots to do in one evening – pretty miserable.

Big heads

Heads are the most important people at your school. They can be so nice but can come down on you like a ton of bricks, so be careful how you treat them. They are totally responsible for all the other teachers, you and your behaviour and achievements. A good Head means a good school. Some schools are lucky, some are not. Fortunately for me I came from a school with a great Headmaster, full of fun and he passed this on to us. His jokes were legendary. **Give your Head massive respect - they can make your life Heaven or Hell!**

Tips for a star pupil

My Head also gave us some tips to be successful in Year 6.

* Be enthusiastic and have a go at everything.

* Try to get on with everyone particularly the different teachers as they are all really nice people deep down!

* Listen more than you speak!

* Be prepared to laugh at yourself.

* Don't be over sensitive or believe people are out to get you, they are not.

* Laugh a lot!

How long

In Years 4 and 5 homework should take about 20/30 minutes a night rising to 30/40 minutes in Year 6. In Year 7 expect upwards of an hour a day. Don't let it build up. Use a planner and spread it over the week. Of course there are always the wicked teachers who overload you and expect homework done for the next day. If it really becomes a problem go and see the teacher and explain or ask for help. No child should spend hours on homework so if this happens regularly the teachers need to know.

Power pointers

PowerPoint is a great way to do school presentations or assemblies. PowerPoint is really easy to use for any age. With PowerPoint you can:

1. Use preformatted templates to help you plug information into slides quickly and professionally.

2. ClipArt can really make a difference to PowerPoint by making it easier to find the best pictures to use.

3. Add graphics that help you insert illustrations with just a few clicks of the mouse.

4. Use different text effects to make the words really stand out.

5. Display your photos; add photo effects and animation to get your point across.

Try it out and I'll guarantee it will put the fun into most of your subjects.

Perfect presentations

Top tips for doing that all important presentation to the class:

- Allow time to research fully before.
- Don't read direct from a script.
- Know you audience and make it interesting for them.
- Have an opening, middle and conclusion.
- Use short sentences and don't mumble or waffle.
- Add a funny story or examples if you have them.
- Rehearse it well.
- Don't shout but keep your head up and speak up.
- Keep eye contact.
- Smile and relax.  SMILE!
- Look at your notes a bit but face the front.

How to write a good letter

School doesn't always teach us how to write a proper letter and texting and e-mail can make us pretty useless.

* Plan what you want to say and who you are saying it to. It could be a thank you note, congratulations or a complaint.

* Put your address in the top right hand corner.

* The date goes under this.

* Dear "whoever" goes on the immediate left.

* Then the main letter and keep to the point.

* Check spelling and grammar.

* Close it with "Love from" if it's a family member etc.

* Or "Best wishes" if you don't know them that well.

* Or "Yours sincerely" if it's a formal letter but you know their name.

* Or "Gratefully" for a thank you letter.

* Postcards can be a nice way to say thank you and if what you want to say is not a secret!

School reports

We all dread the comments that our teachers are going to make about us on our school reports and how our parents will react, but hang on to them. It would be funny to look at them when we're grown up to see if the teachers were right about us. Myself? I doubt it!

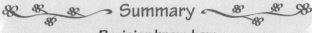

Summary

Revision know-how

- Make important dates, phrases etc. stand out with highlighter pens or colours.

- Make fun songs to help you remember your phrases.

- Pick your subject and then break it down into headings and write each heading in a list on a sheet of paper. Cross off each heading as you revise it so you can see what progress you are making.

- There are lots of different ways to revise and each person does it in their own special way. Some people use flash cards or post-it notes, some read and then write it all down.

- Try not to watch so much TV the night before your exam otherwise you'll be tired. Get a good night's sleep and a good breakfast too.

- Practise previous papers.

- Stick to your plan.

chapter 4
Safety & survival

How do bees get to school?
On the school buzz!

Here are my tips to help you be a bit more mature, careful and responsible while enjoying school to the full, keeping out of trouble and staying safe...

Two way traffic

Always give your parents the letters they are supposed to get from your school. They need to know the dates you break up, go back to school, sports fixtures, parents' evenings and other important dates. This always makes it easier for them to book things around your school life.

Shhhh

If you are going to have your mobile phone with you at school always check to see if it's on silent. You don't want it going off in class or worse in assembly.

Luk b4 u txt

Your school will have rules about mobiles but a lot of them will be common sense. If you send anyone abusive text messages or phone calls it is a criminal offence and I'm sure your school will find out and deal with it seriously. If anything horrible about someone else is written then they are bound to find out, so think before you text. If you happen to receive a nasty message first show it to someone you trust like your parents or teacher to get their opinion, before you show your friends and it goes around the whole school. You could always be mature, ignore it and press the delete button.

Phone safety

 We all have our favourite numbers saved in our phone memory. Save an additional one under **E for "Emergency"**. This should be who to call in case of accident or emergency if you are unable to communicate yourself.

Paper copy

Disaster! You lose your phone and all contact numbers with it. Make sure you have the details on paper at home of all your mates' numbers or you will be lost as well as the phone. You can save them to your computer if you know how!

Pocket wise

When travelling to and from school, carry your house keys in one pocket and your mobile phone in the other. That way if the worst happens and your school bag is snatched you can still call the police and get in the house. If you do ever lose your mobile it's good to know your parents' numbers off by heart.

Chit chat

There are a lot of internet chat rooms where you can talk with other people who share your interests. Give yourself a nickname but don't use the same one as you use for your email address, this is so people don't know your real name. Make sure that your parents have installed filtering software on your home PC as this is the best way for them to protect you from internet predators in chat rooms.

Mobile phone safety

A mobile phone is stolen in Britain every 3 minutes. So look after yours, it could be at risk.

- Try to keep your phone hidden where it can't be seen and don't use it on the street.

- You will be less of a target for a robbery on a street, if you put your phone on vibrate when you are out .

- Never walk and talk on the phone.

- If you are threatened with violence for anyone demanding your phone, hand it over; it is only a phone after all. You can always get a new one.

Confidence coach

- Always try to mix with the kids in class who make you feel good about yourself; this helps your own self-image.

- Try and stay focused on what you want to gain from your life. Write down a picture of what your ideal life would be and all that you hope to achieve and look at it from time to time.

- We all need goals in life, however big or small, to give us purpose. If you think about doing big things you're more likely to go for it and maybe end up doing it as your job when you're older.

- Keep it realistic, write down a plan and tackle it in achievable steps. Then you'll do whatever you want.

Coping with death

Losing someone is never easy, whether it is a friend or a member of your family. It is one of the toughest things you'll ever have to go through. If someone dies what you go through is called bereavement and it could happen to you or one of your school friends. It is important that you recognise your feelings, let them out and deal with them. Bottling up emotions and trying to act like everything is fine can cause problems when you are older.

Whether it is you or your friends, the following tips will help.

1. The sad feelings are normal and can last a long time and everyone deals with it in their own different way. Help your friends by talking about their memories of the person who has died or just give them space and time to come to terms with it.

2. If you or your friends are finding it difficult to cope at school explain the situation to the teacher. They will understand.

3. Try to let all of your close friends know what's happened and let them know what they can do to help, even if that's just being normal. Tell them it is okay to talk and that sometimes you will want to have fun with them.

4. If you are the one left behind, no matter how upset and sad you feel make sure you continue to eat healthily and keep yourself clean and get the right amount of sleep and exercise.

5. We have prefects at our school, if you have them you should feel comfortable talking to them about anything that is bothering you either at home or at school.

6. At my school we also have a buddy system, these are like prefects but you can choose who you would like to speak to. They are 6th Formers and have been trained especially to listen and help you.

Pick-up Password

Make sure you always know how, when, where and who is picking you up from school or your extra activities. Pick a password that only you and your parents know (this can be something like you nanna`s name, Mum's middle name). If your parents send someone to collect you they should be told the it so you can confirm the password with them.

Grades and badges

Everyone loves a badge or a certificate. These can be for many things, most commonly music, sport and academic exams. In music, grades are an important measurement of the standard you have reached. A good level in say piano or violin will get you a long way if you want to get into a particular school which specialises in music. Being at county standard at say rugby or tennis will help you get selected for a sports academy school. Same goes for college or university when you're older.

First warnings

Most children don't get through a year (or even a week) without a warning. These can be given for talking in class, not giving homework in on time, or poor work. OK nobody's perfect and who would want to be, but take notice of them as the next time the punishment will be more severe and you have been warned.

De-merits or bad behaviour slips

These come as a result of serious misconduct — passing notes, fighting and cheek or even minor things if the teacher is in a really bad mood!

Take note that your parents are likely to find out if this happens a lot and worse, you will be letting the side down as you can lose many house points every time it happens.

Money, money, money

Most of us have been money mad from an early age, saving it in a money box, jar or bank account. We all learn about it as we go, from being in the supermarket, looking on eBay and just listening to parents going on about it. Knowing what money can buy is only half the story. What is more important is the value of it. So how can we be a bit wiser about money?

Take a look at the different prices of articles by comparing like for like around the shops when you are with your friends, or looking for different brands. Maybe set yourselves a task of all buying the same make of deodorant or shampoo one week and see who got it the cheapest. Do it over a month and chart the results. It may give you a shock as well as more money to spend.

Richer or poorer

Years 6 and 7 are notorious for an obsession with who is rich and who is not. This is shown in the competition to have the best birthday party or designer clothes. Well there will always be the spoilt kids who seem to get everything they

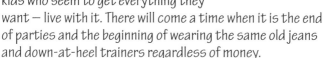

want – live with it. There will come a time when it is the end of parties and the beginning of wearing the same old jeans and down-at-heel trainers regardless of money.

Try to take a good look behind the flashy clothes and see what is important. You only have to look at the TV appeals for money for kids in Africa and **Children in Need** to see that we all really do have enough. For many people money is a worry, others will never struggle, so try to see your friends for what they bring to you – fun, support, help and laughter and don't let the way they dress or flash money about influence you.

When organising fun activities always remember that some cannot afford certain things, and vary things to include everyone. Cinema and bowling is OK once in a while but hanging out at home with maybe a sports day in the garden or baking etc. can be even better.

Money power

Pocket money is a way of making us that bit independent and pay rises can be given every birthday. Research shows that boys are overtaking the girls by receiving that bit more and on average get 80p more a week. However we are not talking megabucks here with about £5-£10 a week being the norm for ages 11-16.

So apart from chatting up Granny how can we increase the funds we all need? Well part-time jobs may suit some of us, with a paper round being the most popular. The rest of us are encouraged (to put it nicely) or forced into household chores, babysitting, dog walking or car washing. As we go up the school ladder this drops off as the need for general lounging-about exceeds the need for cash from hard work.

Girls are supposed to be worse at getting up in the morning than boys, but are definitely better at spending. Boys are said to be more likely to save than girls. So what does the money go on? Boys favour sportswear and computer games while girls go for all the C's: clothes, cosmetics and CDs... so no surprise there. Most of us knew this without an expensive survey!

Extra cash

Most of us have a friendly bank manager from an early age — our parents. But what they see as a waste of money to us can be an absolute essential. Getting used to pocket money or an allowance can be a good way of keeping Mum or Dad happy and learning the value of money at the same time, because as they always tell us "when it's gone, it's gone".

Of course you can always try for extra by earning it, and Dads love a bit of flattery. It's worth offering to wash the dishes or the car, polish shoes or tidy your room if there's a reward in sight. Mum may have other ideas though and for her these may be pay-free zones. I find offering to make a cup of tea goes down well for an advance on pocket money, do it with a smile and the rewards can be high!

Top tip

You pop to the toilet by yourself and there is no toilet roll – what on earth do you do? You can't ask anyone for some paper. What you need to do is check before you go in that cubicle, or just plain and simply ALWAYS carry round some tissues so you don't have to worry about having the 'stranded' problem.

Give something back

Whatever money we do have, just buying this book proves that you will possibly have more than many. So give something back. There's the **Race for Life** and various sponsored local fun runs that will do the paperwork for you in return for your sponsor money. Or hold a table top sale or car boot sale to off-load all of your old toys and clothes. If that's not possible then take them along to your local charity shop who will ensure the money goes to the charity of your choice.

Learn first aid as you never know when you will be needed in a crisis or get up a group of friends to join you at a retirement home over Christmas to sing carols. Every little thing means so much to others and once in a while may make you stop and think how lucky we are.

The art of interviews

Look more serious in interviews or debates — they will start happening as you progress through senior school. When you are talking lean in towards the centre of the table looking the interviewer in the eye. Then, when people are putting their ideas to you, lean back and look casual. Don't smile too much, don't cross and uncross your legs or play with your hair and this will mean you've got the serious advantage in the room.

Looking good

Not everyone is the best in the class, that is impossible, and some people just aren't good at some subjects but you don't have to tell others that. Give the impression that you are clever and carry a really intelligent book around with you. Take Paris Hilton and Lindsay Lohan – not exactly the brightest in the bunch but with a book in their hands it's a different story.

Gum

Chewing gum has a disgusting way of attaching itself to your school clothes, and parents just don't listen to the excuses that it's always someone else's fault. Get it off school trousers or skirts by rubbing on white vinegar. It will break up and fall away. It's is slightly better to smell of vinegar all day than walk around with a blob of chewy on your front.

Don't pass that note

A lot of people pass notes in class, they are never necessary and usually done out if sheer boredom. It's easy to be roped in, particularly if you are on the receiving end and it's not good form to expose it, but don't be tempted to join in. Always beware that they are likely to be read out for all to hear and it's "kid's law" that the ones read out will be the worst. Rude stuff, back-stabbing your mates, confidential info will always find it's way into the public domain and that's a recipe for trouble (not only with the teacher but with your friends).

Here are two funny examples:

"See you tonight at my house; Mum's left the door keys in the rabbit hutch."

If this got read out, a piece of top secret information has just been given away, let's hope no-one knows where you live.

Here's another example of a different type of note:

"Have you seen that huge spot on Lewis's nose? It's gross, I don't like him anyway."

That would be awful if read out — you would possibly lose friends too.

The bard

Memorise a few famous quotes from Shakespeare and slip them in at the right time and they will leave people stunned! Here's some for starters:

"Et tu Bruté" from Julius Caesar — good when a friend lets you down.

"Double, double toil and trouble" from Macbeth — good when teachers are on the prowl.

"Goodnight, parting is such sweet sorrow" from Romeo and Juliet.

"To be or not to be, that is the question" from Hamlet.

School photo

Every few years your school will have a school photo with everybody in it. They are great if you look back after a long time but I bet you won't remember people's names. So when you get it why don't you write the names on the back of the photo, then a few years on you will remember everyone's names?

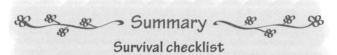

Summary
Survival checklist

Consider...

* What you text and e-mail may come back on you.

* Keep your phone, keys and money safe.

* Watch out for strangers on land and in cyberspace.

* Impress the teachers but don't cheek them.

* Give something back to others when you can.

chapter 5
On the ball

Mum: What did you learn in school today?
Son: Not enough, I have to go back tomorrow!

I have always enjoyed sport at school but many do not. It is not always their fault and can be down to poor teachers or loss of confidence. I hope that these tips will help you join in, enjoy it more and learn that there's something for everyone even if you are not in the first team. School sport and fitness training can teach us all lessons that are just as important as our written ones, like social and communication skills, how to concentrate better, co-ordination and self-confidence. That's got to be better than sitting at your desk all day!

On your feet

Statistics show that only half of 11-16 year-olds manage to walk for even 10 minutes a day and children in Britain overall walk 50 miles a year less then they did 10 years ago. In many schools the amount of sport we do has dropped. British schools are said to do less P.E. than most other European countries, so get up and get exercising.

Walking is really good for your heart and lungs but it is also really good for your muscles and bones. So get together with your friends and walk to school, walk at weekends and not just walk round the shops. Walking is also great for socialising and you will tend to open up more to your friends while sharing a joint activity and this is especially true for boys. If you have a dog you have no excuse not to walk everyday.

Walking is completely free and you don't need any special equipment at all, as long as you don't go for a hike in a pair of brand new stilettos. You should wear trainers or walking boots if you have any.

When you go walking you can get really cold, so instead of wearing a little T-shirt put on a few layers. You can always take a layer off but be realistic – you don't want to be carrying lots of jumpers with you. This doesn't just apply to walking it could be for anything, hockey, netball, tennis etc.

Fitness fun

Not everyone can get picked for the school sports teams. You could miss out and certainly some of your friends will, but this doesn't mean that you can't get together and get fit. It can be something like riding your bike around the local park with your friends and you don't need expensive equipment or a personal trainer to get fit. Choose your favourite exercise and repeat it or try out lots of different activities until you all find the ones that suit you best. Or go for a swim at your local pool.

This is cheap and available to everyone. If you and your friends just have fun then you won't realise that you are actually exercising. Pop round to a friend's and have a girlie day in, working out to an exercise DVD. This is much cheaper than signing up for classes and can be more fun. The secret to fitness is fun and there is no doubt that getting your friends to join you for an exercise session is much more enjoyable than pounding the streets on your own.

Nice moves

Hoola hoops have suddenly become the latest craze again. It's really fun, easy and you lose weight on your thighs, waist and your bum. Dance mats are really fun to do; you can keep fit, learn the latest dance moves, sing along and most importantly enjoy.

Help fight cancer

Every year, thousands of females from all over the UK have taken part in Cancer Research UK's Race for Life. Yes, kids of all ages can join together to run this race either with their Mums and family members or as a group. Visit www.raceforlife.com and find out how you can get fit and raise money for a worthy cause. It's honestly really fun, my friends and I all did it in our pajamas.

The great outdoors

Instead of staying inside at lunch breaks at school get out of school even if it is only for a stroll around the school playground or field. This will help clear your head and give your muscles a much-needed stretch. In winter the dark days can make some people feel sad or low so getting out can give them that well-deserved lift to make them feel much better.

Wet and wild

If you're heading for an outdoor attraction with the school, don't forget to put your wellies, coat, and umbrella in the bus just in case. You never know what the weather is going to be like in Britain. It's handy to pack a change of clothes too (little accidents can happen when you least expect it) and taking some wet wipes would be a good idea. Make sure that you take lots of food and drink with you, us kids are always hungry and it's good if you don't have to pay for food every 5 minutes.

Weekend workout

We all know the kids' law — that it is easier to get up early at the weekend than during the week. Make the most of that extra time and energy by making the weekend different. Head straight out the door and offer to get the papers or walk the dog. This will make you mentally more alert and a brisk walk gets the exercise for the day done and dusted. You will even feel you deserve that fry up Mum has made you when you come in. But now you are set up for the day DON'T WASTE IT! Weekdays are for school work and weekends are for enjoying.

Write down just what you achieved the weekend before, my bet is that you just drifted along filling up the time sleeping, watching TV, sitting at the computer while that precious time disappeared.

Now you know where the time flew, get it back.

- Get all homework out of the way on Friday night, making the weekend yours.

- Plan on Friday for the weekend, What will the weather do? What friends are around? What family commitments do you have like parties or visiting relatives?

- How can you help make them more fun? Can you organise games for the little ones in the family, do a quiz for everyone or direct a play or show for Granny?

- Do something different — go swimming, help cook Sunday lunch or even go mad and actually have a go at reading the Sunday paper.

Calorie counter

Which sport helps you burn up the most calories in 1 hour?

Cycling (faster than 10mph)	510
Running with a backpack	490
Squash	450
Football	430
Roller-skating	413
Badminton	360
Netball	330
Table tennis	315
Skateboarding	295

So get going!

Leadership

Good leaders are NEVER bossy but praise, encourage and motivate other players.

Jolly journeys

If you get picked for the school team you sometimes have to go to away fixtures and this can mean long coach journeys. It's not just fixtures though, if you ever have to go on a school trip there are lots of things you can do with your spare time to keep you occupied. Try these:

1. A pack of ordinary playing cards will provide loads of games as well as specialist games like Uno.

2. Take a pen and some paper – you can do lots of different games keeping you occupied for ages.

3. Take a magazine and do the quizzes that are in there as well as the crossword.

4. Make sure you actually know where you are going and how long it's going to take you to get there.

5. You can always read a book or do your homework on the coach but not if you suffer from travel sickness as this will definitely make it worse. If you do get travel sick you can take some travel sickness tablets or wear special wristbands, you don't want to be sick before a day out or a match.

6. Take a camera (disposable ones are good) and take pictures of your friends as they are snoring on the coach. Always nice to show them after the event.

7. 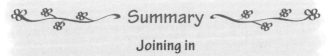 It's always nice to listen to music so take your iPod, mp3 player etc.

Summary

Joining in

Not everyone is good at sport and not everyone likes it. But these days there is something for everyone in most schools and it is very important for all kids to do some form of exercise to keep fit and healthy. So try and find something that suits you. This does not have to mean being in a team or competing.

Many sports are individual challenges. These can be: Trampolining, Swimming, Gymnastics, Dance, Aerobics and Jogging.

Most schools will have A, B, C and even D teams in order to involve everyone who wants to take part — not just the best. So join in, have a go, you are bound to be better than you think especially with practice. Remember even out of the best school players very few become professionals. All sport should be about having fun.

chapter 6
Beat the bullies

What sleeps at the bottom of the sea?
A kipper!

What is bullying?

Childline is a brilliant charity and the website is in the back of this book. They say bullying can mean different things to different people. They have spoken to many kids who have described bullying as:

- Being called names.
- Being teased.
- Being pushed about.
- Being hit, bitten or pinched.
- Having your things thrown about or stolen.
- Having rumours or lies spread or written about you.
- Being left out or ignored continually.
- Having your friends taken away from you.
- Being forced to hand over money or possessions.
- Being called names because of your religion or colour.

Whatever it is, it hurts. It makes you scared and upset and affects your schoolwork and relationships. Some children skip school just because of bullies and it's hard for them to go back and face them.

Bullies make you feel that it's your entire fault and you are to blame and you can feel stupid or no good as a person.
IT IS NOT YOU FAULT – BE BRAVE – GET HELP – GET IT SORTED.

Involve the experts

If you go to the school with your parents the teachers will have seen this many times and have inside knowledge to help you. So listen to them even if you think you know best and these tips are for the whole family:

- Practise what you want to say before you go and stay calm.

- Ask the staff what they think is the best action to take.

- Make sure the Headteacher is aware of it all.

- Put it in writing if you feel it is necessary and ask for it to be kept on file.

- If things get worse start a diary and record all the events, times, dates etc.

- Ask to see the school's policy on bullying and complain if you believe that you are not being taken seriously.

- Ask them to keep a watch over any meetings/lessons between the children involved.

- Follow it up by checking back with the school about what they have done to control the situation.

The NSPCC have excellent advice on line if it all goes too far or too wrong.

Technology nightmares

Text messaging and e-mail bullying is on the increase and is now one of the main ways kids can be excluded, picked on and frightened. If you are tempted to join in the name calling game, gossip or nastiness then you will be caught out in writing! Often you will be left carrying the can for the one that started it — leaving you as the victim. So don't get involved as the evidence will be there to catch you. You may not like it but parents should monitor all cyberspace behaviour and see just what is going on out there.

Cyber-bullies

Even the government has seen that hi-tech bullying is out there and has issued tips for schools on this. However we can help ourselves by:

- Never answering abusive e- mails.

- Deleting all nasty texts immediately or showing an adult first, but never forwarding them on or replying.

- Never using chat rooms unless in a public controlled place like at school or home under supervision.

- Never giving out our addresses or sending photos online.

Mirror confidence

Beating the bullies at their own game takes a lot of confidence and skill but you can learn this, however daft you may feel at first...

1. Practise saying "No" or "Leave me alone" in the mirror.

2. Imagine some of the things they say like "You are fat" and reply with "Thank you".

3. Then think about how your own voice sounds when you are scared. Is it quieter?

4. Then see how it sounds when you are comfortable and happy, because this is the voice you have to let the bullies have — strong loud and clear.

5. Using the confident voice stand in front of the mirror and say "I am a confident person", "I love going out to play or to school" and "I am a really nice person".

Role models

Can you think of someone who you look up to, admire or is talented in a way you would like to be? It could be a friend, sports personality or TV star — we all know them. They will be the confident one who has succeeded in some way big or small. It may be the star of the school play or a teacher, right up to a premiership footballer. But they were not born like that. They will have learned it from someone as their mentor or role model and then practised it till they became good at it. So watch how they do it and pick up on the way they talk and walk.

Help at hand

Expert help is listed at the back of the book. I have read it to help me with these tips.

Talking is the answer. Speak to your family, your teachers or an adult you know and trust. Be honest about what is happening but don't exaggerate. A problem shared is a problem halved and most situations are quickly solved.

Your school will have a Bullying Policy which will have been tried and tested, meaning they will have dealt with these problems many times. You will not be the first. If you feel threatened by a bully, go in head held high and look them in the eye and give as good as you get in a non-confrontational way.

Stick with the friends who love you for what you are and ignore the rest! Bullies hate to be ignored as they thrive on attention so make sure that you never laugh at their jokes. Look out for others who may be the victims of a bully and help them as you would like to be helped urself.

chapter 7
The xtra factors

Who invented fractions?
Henry the 1/8!

School's not just about education and you will discover lots of out-of-school and lunch-time activities for you to try. Go for them, they are free and help you decide what you want from school and life. You may start something and then drop it but don't worry you will have still gained something from trying it out. A good part of school is what you do outside of it with your school friends. School doesn't end at 4 o'clock at the school gate so read on for tips on how to get more out of life.

Lunchtime fun

Join in as many lunchtime clubs as you can. These can be sport (or fitness), arts and crafts, IT, DT, hobbies like chess or music.

The music clubs are a great way of getting a free lesson from the teachers in say a string group, orchestra, quartet, choir or band. These things usually cost money nowadays at most schools. Also it means you get to improve in school by playing with friends and this cuts down the practising needed at home.

Sports clubs are more laid back than lesson time and mean all can belong and not just the stars.

All clubs are a great way to make friends outside of your usual peer group or class. The teachers will get to know you better too in a more relaxed setting where they are using their specialist skills and enjoying passing them on to you — in other words showing off!

Never forget

Time after school and at weekends can be used to go along to clubs and activities run by the school. This may be competing against other schools in sport, travelling with your choir or orchestra or on camping, skiing or adventure holidays. These are the things you most remember from schooldays.

Ask your parents what they remember and it will definitely be that trip to France or day out at the seaside – usually when some mischief took place! But it's a great opportunity so take it if you can. All schools have help available for those families who can't always afford trips and it is done in secret, so have fun, you will never forget it.

Sleepover dos and don'ts

Do

* Warn parents about what you might be doing.

* Provide sweets and treats at midnight.

* Be prepared for a few secrets and gossip to come out! (You will be the subject of it at someone else's!)

* Provide food for all tastes (veggies, allergies, religion).

* Restrict it to 4 people because
  * 2`s = good company.
  * 3`s = an odd number which equals an odd one out.
  * 4`s = something for all/you will never be lonely.

- Send invites to all to check that they can come and can be involved in the preparation.

- RSVP – this mean reply soon as possible or by a certain date.

- Maybe have a theme like makeovers or DVDs or a school project and bring everything needed.

- Show them the main places they will need in your house like the toilet, your room, the kitchen and the drinks fridge.

- Tell them to be aware of the burglar alarm in the night so if they sleepwalk they don't set it off!

Don't

- Get too involved in all the arguments or nastiness.

- Have sleepovers if you have to get to school the next day for 8.30 am!

- Moan if you have netball/football etc. the next morning.

- Send horrid msn messages.

- Let anyone in unless they're invited!

- Give out medicines without parental consent – maybe they have allergies etc.

- Leave electrical items on overnight, i.e. straighteners, TV, DVD player etc.

- Be bossy, as you might not get invited to their next sleepover.

Get wrapping

Instead of buying lots of wrapping paper to wrap Christmas and birthday presents how about making your own wrapping paper using colourful magazines or decorate plain paper yourself. It might look a bit weird at first but you could easily set a trend. Then wrap the present with real ribbon rather than plastic ribbon. Although it costs more it can be reused lots of times and can come in useful for other things.

Don't drop it – bin it

A lot of schools have a litter problem in one way or another. This can give a bad impression to visitors at your school. Some litter can be very dangerous to pupils or wildlife in your school. Your school should tackle the problem, if it doesn't you should just pick it up and put it in the bin or better recycle it.

Scrapbooks

When something happens in your life you may like to remember it and maybe diaries aren't your thing. So why not make a scrapbook? Record dates and times and people's names, stick in pictures and scraps of paper with things on that you'd like to remember. This isn't expensive and can all be done with recycled products.

Lose it – use it

Paper that has been recycled not only has great green brownie points but makes extremely good use of our most common waste products. Use it.

Cut the cards

At Christmas don't send the usual 50 or 60 Christmas cards to all your friends and get them in return but just send a great email to all your friends and family instead. You can then make a donation of a few pounds to a local charity instead of what you would spend on the cards themselves. If you have to buy cards, buy the ones from a charity which appeals to you.

Cheap and cheerful

Birthday parties can be very expensive and it becomes a competition about who does the best party. It's a nightmare for Mums and Dads.

A good idea for a girlie party is to invite your friends over for a makeover party. Decide which of you will do the manicure, the pedicure, the facial, and the massage. All you have to provide is the nail polish, creams and oils. These can be given as party bags at the beginning of the party and what's left taken home. Put on some music or DVD's and ask Mum to lay on some sandwiches etc. The good friends are what you want to have, not the vast expense some dos can cost. Just think the money saved can go towards your present!

Thanks

Most people have had parties before and have probably had to spend ages writing out thank you letters and the people that have done this will know what I mean when I say it takes for ever. So to save yourself from spending hours writing them, go on your computer and write something like: "Thanks for my card and gift, it is really nice and very thoughtful of you."

You can copy these as many times as you need and put them in the party bags or give them out as people leave. This way people are happy and it saves you lots of time after the party's over.

Secret Santa

When Christmas comes at school it can cost a bomb so why not do a Secret Santa? If you don't know what this is, it's a way of all your friends getting a present but each person only buys one. Everybody's name goes into box, or hat (or something like that) on paper and then everyone picks one name in secret and buys for that person. You all agree on a price and then at Christmas you give the presents out.

Promises promises

At Christmas and birthdays it can cost the earth to give all of your friends a present and you don't want to appear mean. Why not all get together and organise an exchange of promises. Everyone has things they are just not good at or hate doing – but you may love them. Things like:

* Doing an hour's help with maths homework.
* Typing up work.
* Cleaning football boots.
* Doing packed lunches.
* Wake-up calls in a morning.
* Walking to school with someone.
* Testing for exam revision.
* Sewing name tapes on or hems up.
* Dog walking/horse grooming.
* Teach them trampolining or knitting.

Join the green party

Thinking of having your usual birthday party? Try to keep it eco-friendly as well as fun by having it at home and doing your own food and drink, and why not bake your own cake using organic ingredients? Your friends could help you ice it in your special way before the party if you could keep your hands off it that long. Here's a couple more green ideas.

Recycle it

 If you must send invitations make sure they are on recycled paper or make your own from old cards. The party could leave you with a bin full of waste wrapping paper and boxes so tell your friends not to wrap your present, but tell them to spend more on it instead!

For party bags use recycled, reusable or bio-degradable ones if you must. Everyone gets the odd present that they don't like or don't need, so instead of throwing it away give it to someone else for their birthday. Just make sure not to give it to the person that gave you it in the first place.

Knit

There is only one way to be warm when winter arrives and it involves wool, learn to knit on www.youtube.co.uk. You could even start a knitting circle or just get your granny to teach you.

Swap

Sign up at www.bigwardrobe.com to trade your unwanted clothes, you could also check out www.swishing.org or sell them on eBay.

Scary readers

Get right out the comfort zone and buy or borrow a book that you would never normally try. Look at the shop's recommended titles for your age group as good book shops will guide you in the right direction, or view titles on the internet. If lots of kids recommend something they can't all be wrong! When you have read a good book pass it on. Think about setting up a book sharing club at school and meet once a month to swap books.

If you are really adventurous a book reading club is that step further. Choose a book which you all agree to read over say a month. Meet in your lunch break or at a friend's house in the evening and share thoughts about the book, your likes and dislikes. Someone could always write a review too for the school magazine — if that's not going too far!

Passport peril

If you are going abroad with the school, take a photocopy of your passport with you as well as the original. Keep it in a separate place from the original. Or try scanning your passport and emailing it to yourself before you leave. If you lose your passport you can access your email and print off a copy or show your photocopy to help you get a replacement very quickly.

Going camping

 Practise putting the tent up in your garden before you go, remember don't put it away damp or it will come out mouldy.

Warm up with a flask

Got your flask out but it stinks of old soup? Fill it up with warm water and two of great grannie's denture cleaning tablets and leave overnight. This gets rid of any awful smells from your flask.

Travelling light

Once you've got all your gear laid out for a school trip then halve it! You have to carry it!

Stick to the list.

- Choose a very lightweight bag.
- Clean undies daily are a must – clean jeans are not.
- Roll up clothes to prevent creases and save space.
- Stuff shoes.
- Wear the bulkiest items to travel in.
- Save on underwear by washing out at night (remember to take some pegs).
- Buy your toiletries when you get there to lighten the load.

Guides

You can find out about the Girl Guides and Scouts from the Internet or your friends – but did you know that if you are between 10 and 14 the Guides can mean travel and excitement. It's a way to make new friends out of school where you can look out for others as they will do for you. So if you fancy the outdoor life camping or abseiling down a local landmark check out their website. Scouts go from 6 to 25 and involve teamwork and taking acceptable risks and that's excitement. Reach your full potential outside of school with your local Scout group.

Walking

A cheap way to see the country, keep fit and bond with friends and family is to set off for a long walk. Following a trail travelled by many before you can give you real sense of achievement. Try The Pennine Way (not all 268 miles of it) from the Peak District to Hadrian's Wall or for the hardier of you read up on the Lyke Wake Walk. It's 40 miles in 24 hours of North Yorkshire Moors from East to West. You will need a good group leader and a lot of practice and may not make it before Year 10 but it's worth working towards.

Cadets

There are The Sea Cadets, Air Cadets and Army Cadets often run through your school giving great preparation to youths over the age of 12 or 13.

The Army Cadet Force has over 44,000 young people across the UK all encouraged to help local communities. The Sea Cadets will enable you to learn new skills from mainly waterborne activities, whilst the Air Cadets will give flying opportunities and offer expeditions across the UK and even further afield.

Duke of Edinburgh Awards

This is an award scheme for you to do in your spare time. There are 3 levels, Bronze Silver and Gold. Starting at Bronze you can learn a new skill from the flying trapeze to sculpture, get active with sport or dance, plan a journey on foot, wheels or horseback and learn real team work. It is challenging but why not take the challenge there's no such word as bored in it!

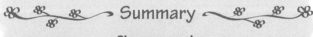
Class capsule

To make sure you remember the good times why not make a class capsule and put in it what you want? It could include:

- Year 6 and 7 class photos with names on the back.

- Name of your best friend.

- The name of the person you didn't like.

- An item of clothing like an old school shirt or tie signed by your mates.

- Copy of grade card or school report.

- Any school trip or play photos.

When you have done this hide it in an attic and get it out on your last day of school in Year 13 and see what you were like back then.

Teacher: "Name two days beginning with T."

Pupil: "Today and tomorrow!"

chapter 8

Pass it to parents

What's the definition of an adult?

A person who has stopped growing at both ends but started growing in the middle!

Parents beware

Us kids don't always tell our Mums and Dads about what's going on at school for many reasons and sometimes we may not realise that we are actually being bullied. We may even think it's normal or we deserve it. So how can family or those close to us recognise it and help us? The signs will be there and might be:

- Being even moodier than normal – snappy and withdrawn.

- Staying awake all night with the TV or computer on.

- Being aggressive or nasty to other children in the family or displaying jealousy to them.

- Losing dinner money, bus money or lunch.

- Losing games kit or coming home with clothes damaged or torn.

- Refusing to go to school or missing lessons.

Of course as soon as an adult queries this your child may start acting up even more, so parents beware, you will be angry and want to take sides but don't jump in too quick with the questions or answers – talk it over and go to school, get the facts from all sides and take it from there.

Parent pointers

Here are a few helpful hints for Mum and Dad to help you get you through the evening's homework.

1. Don't let the child leave homework until just before bedtime.

2. Let kids use a weekend to work on big projects especially if this involves getting together with their classmates. If they do it on a school night it will take a long time, and they miss out on other activities or other homework.

3. Tell your child how important school is.

4. Maybe read at the same time as the child is reading to show them support.

5. If your child asks for help, provide guidance not answers.

6. Co-operate with the teacher and show the child that the school and home are a team.

7. Homework is a way for kids to develop lifelong learning skills so, if homework is meant to be done by the child, keep out of it.

8. Let your child take a short break if they are having trouble keeping their mind on homework. If they struggle maybe contact the teacher about the problem.

9. Follow their progress but don't be surprised if you can't do it yourself.

Parent power

Parents or guardians can help by supporting a child in many ways through problems at school without judging them and with an open mind and here are some tips:

- Let the child know that they have your support always and that you are there to listen (without butting in) not easy for most Mums!

- Tell them that you will *do* something about it calmly as many kids think that involving Mum or Dad will make it far worse for them.

- Remember if the child then becomes more clingy that it's normal after a nasty experience.

- Tell the child to stick with their *good* mates and carry on as normal.

- And encourage them to go to as many outside activities as they can to keep occupied and fit.

- Never give up even when you think a problem is over. Keep an eye out in case it starts up again as it often can do.

Online safety tips for parents

1. Honestly all you should spend on the computer is about one hour a day.

2. People not computers should be your child's best friends so help them to find a balance between computing and other outdoor activities.

3. Always keep the computer in the family room, never in the child's bedroom. They could go on anything if you are not there. Don't be afraid to check the screen regularly to make sure that they are viewing appropriate material, but don't destroy the child's trust. Let them show you that they have the good judgement to know right from wrong.

4. Nowadays children will know more than their parents about computers so learn about computers yourself so that you can enjoy them together with your children.

5. Make sure you know who your child is speaking to get to know your child's online friends just as you know their other friends. Ask them who is on their list of contacts and who they talk to most frequently. You will then get a feel for what's happening.

6. Help your children to set up their email accounts and spam filters and encourage them to tell you if they have any problems.

7. Teach your children never to download programmes, fill forms in or download music or files without your permission. File sharing can be illegal.

8. Get your kids to create passwords with a mixture of numbers and letters as these are the first line of defence in protecting your computer from criminals. If you don't use a password to log on anyone can access your computer and unlock it.

Messy messages

Your kids should only talk to people they know online. This way they can trust those people not to steal any of their private information. If they receive messages that they don't want they must not be afraid to tell you. Make sure you have regular chats to your kids about what they are doing online.

And here are some tips for Mum and Dad:

1. Make sure the kids don't use the Internet too much and don't let them be in chat rooms for long — especially at night.

2. If you discover that they've looked at something you consider inappropriate then don't be afraid to take it up with them.

3. If they receive phone calls, mail or presents from people you don't know, ask them about this immediately.

4. If they make local or long distance calls to numbers you don't recognise, check this out on your phone bills and talk about it with them.

5. When you go in the bedroom, if they immediately minimise or close a programme or website or shut off their computer monitor, ask why and make sure you do look into it.

6. Don't be afraid to look through their messages, most of it will be harmless fun but there are dangers all around for children.

Expert parents

It's nice that Mum and Dad want to come along to cheer for you on the sidelines and whilst Dad may have been "county standard" in his day, do you really want them shouting advice and embarrassing you in front of your friends. It will happen, it's part of the job description for them, but here's a few tips to pass on to them to make the day go your way:

1. Clap quietly.

2. Don't boast to friend's parents about how the teacher says you are the best kid in the team (even if it is true).

3. Don't argue with the ref.

4 Don't criticise other players or comment on the fat kids as their parents may be behind you.

5. Don't tell the other dads that you were "county standard". I mention this again as my Dad constantly tells everyone this at any opportunity. It can get boring.

6. Don't turn up in new white trainers/shell suit.

7. Don't wear anything too young/too old fashioned/too bright/too short or any headgear whatsoever.

8. Don't approach the teacher with complaints or praise, just blend into the background.

9. Definitely do not wave during a game.

10. Wait in the car after the whistle has blown and get the food out.

If they play the game your way you will be only too pleased to see them next time.

Summary

We love you really but you can be so embarrassing!

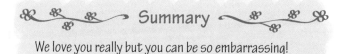

Teacher: You copied from Jake's exam paper didn't you?

Pupil: How did you know?

Teacher: Jake's paper says "I don't know" and you have put "Me neither"!

chapter 9
Checklists & conversions

Did you hear about the cross-eyed teacher?
He couldn't control his pupils!

The following are a few checklists and tables that I found useful but could never put my hand on in a hurry. Keeping this book in your school bag means that you'll always have them handy.

Tool kit

The following items come in handy for the disasters of everyday school life. Try carrying them in a school bag zip pocket, pencil case, favourite tin or something. Replace bits as you use them.

- Tissues — how many times have you been to the toilet and there is no loo roll? Don't get caught it can be very embarrassing.

- Lip salve — (obvious).

- Spare pants — they often fall on the wet floor at swimming or somehow manage to get lost during games (though who would take someone else's pants home I do not know).

- Wet wipes — handy to remove those traces of stray mascara before the teacher sees! Also good for:

  1. Cleaning football boots and trainers.
  2. Freshening up after games.
  3. Wiping up drinks spillages in ICT!
  4. Cleaning up after Art.
  5. Wiping the toilet seat before use — if necessary!
  6. Other unmentionable hygiene uses!

- Hair bobbles — boys and girls keep it tied back for sport and to avoid the nit problem!
- Mini snack bar.
- Plasters.
- Deodorant or deo-wipes.
- Earring tape.
- Empty carrier bag for wet or muddy gear.

Camping checklist

- Tent, pegs and its poles.
- Ground sheet.

- Sleeping bag-pillow, mat.
- Glasses, sunglasses or your contact lenses.
- Sun cream.
- A hat.
- Towel, soap, shampoo, toothpaste and brush.
- Toilet roll (just in case).
- Wet wipes.
- Chocolate bars.
- Torch, batteries.

- Phone.
- Camera.

- Pack of cards.
- Pen and paper.
- Money in purse/wallet.
- Jeans, shorts.
- P.J.s.
- Flip flops for shower.

More adventurous

For an outward bound/activity trip under canvas add more to the above list to keep you dry and safe.

- Rucksack.
- Swimming kit.
- 2/3 extra pairs of old trainers. Save up old trainers well in advance of the trip and be prepared to get them wrecked so that they can be dumped when you leave.
- DO NOT TAKE DESIGNER FOOTWEAR.
- Waterproof coat and trousers.
- Woolly hat and gloves.
- Spare everything i.e. underwear, jeans, tracksuit, socks.
- Wet shoes — rubber pull-on shoes for sailing/canoeing available cheaply from shops, mainly during the summer.
- Medication including travel sickness pills, insect repellent, sunscreen and plasters.

- Decant a little detergent in a small plastic bottle for washing essentials.
- 2 or 3 pegs.
- String.
- Bottled water.
- Whistle.
- Emergency phone numbers and some small change.
- Wellies.
- Walking boots.
- A bag for your dirty clothes.
- Instructions to parents for a hot bath to be ready on your return!

Pupil: "Today my teacher shouted at me for something I didn't do"

Parent: "What was it?"

Pupil: "My homework"

Times tables

Below is a magic chart of timetables up to 10. Everyone will have already learnt their timetables by now, I think, but I still find them tricky sometimes. When you do know them you will never forget them and they are useful throughout life if you learn them well.

Times Table 10 x 10									
	1	2	3	4	5	6	7	8	9	10
1	1	2	3	4	5	6	7	8	9	10
2	2	4	6	8	10	12	14	16	18	20
3	3	6	9	12	15	18	21	24	27	30
4	4	8	12	16	20	24	28	32	36	40
5	5	10	15	20	25	30	35	40	45	50
6	6	12	18	24	30	36	42	48	54	60
7	7	14	21	28	35	42	49	56	63	70
8	8	16	24	32	40	48	56	64	72	80
9	9	18	27	36	45	54	63	72	81	90
10	10	20	30	40	50	60	70	80	90	100

Weights & measure conversions

Length:		
1 millimetre (mm)		= 0.0394 inch (in)
1 centimetre (cm)	= 10 mm	= 0.0394 in
1 metre (m)	= 100 cm	= 1.0936 yard (yd)
1 kilometre (km)	= 1,000 m	= 0.6214 mile

1 inch		= 2.54 cm
1 foot (ft)	= 12 in	= 0.3048 m
1 yard	= 3 ft	= 0.9144 m
1 mile	= 1,760 yd	= 1.6093 km

Area		
1 square cm (cm^2)	= 100 mm^2	= 0.1550 in^2
1 square m (m^2)	= 10,000 cm^2	= 1.1960 yd^2
1 square km (km^2)	= 100 hectares	= 0.3861 mile^2
1 square in (in^2)		= 6.4516 cm^2
1 square ft (ft^2)	= 144 in^2	= 0.0929 m^2
1 square yd (yd^2)	= 9 ft^2	= 0.8361 m^2
1 acre	= 4,840 yd^2	= 4,046.9 m^2
1 square mile (mile^2)	= 640 acres	= 2.590 km^2

Volume		
1 cubic cm (cm^3)		= 0.0610 in^3
1 cubic decimetre (dm^3)	= 1,000 cm^3	= 0.0353 ft^3
1 cubic m (m^3)	= 1,000 dm^3	= 1.3080 yd^3
1 litre (l)	= 1 dm^3	= 1.76 pint (pt)
	= 1000 (ml)	= 2.113 US pt
1 hectolitre (hl)	= 100 l	= 21.997 (gal)
		= 26.417 US gal

1 cubic in (in^3)		= 16.387 cm^3
1 cubic ft (ft^3)	= 1,728 in^3	= 0.0283 m^3
1 cubic yd (yd^3)	= 27 ft^3	= 0.7646 m^3
1 fluid ounce (fl oz)		= 28.413 ml
1 pint (pt)	= 20 fl oz	= 0.5683 l
1 gallon (gal)	= 8 pt	= 4.546 l
		= 1.201 US gal

Mass		
1 milligram (mg)		= 0.0154 grain
1 gram (g)	= 1,000 mg	= 0.0353 oz
1 metric carat	= 0.2 g	= 3.0865 grains
1 kilogram (kg)	= 1,000 g	= 2.2046 lb
1 tonne (t)	= 1,000 kg	= 0.9842 ton
1 ounce (oz)	= 437.5 grains	= 28.35 g
1 pound (lb)	= 16 oz	= 0.4536 kg
1 stone	= 14 lb	= 6.3503 kg
1 hundredweight (cwt)	= 112 lb	= 50.802 kg
1 ton	= 20 cwt	= 1.016 t

Temperature conversions

To convert Fahrenheit to Centigrade:

$C = 5/9 \times (F-32)$

To convert Centigrade to Fahrenheit:

$F = (9/5 \times C) + 32$

Celsius °C	Fahrenheit °F
-30 °C	-22 °F
-20 °C	-4.0 °F
-10 °C	14.0 °F
0 °C	32.0 °F
1 °C	33.8 °F
2 °C	35.6 °F
3 °C	37.4 °F
4 °C	39.2 °F
5 °C	41.0 °F
6 °C	42.8 °F
7 °C	44.6 °F
8 °C	46.4 °F
9 °C	48.2 °F
10 °C	50.0 °F
11 °C	51.8 °F

Celsius °C	Fahrenheit °F
12 °C	53.6 °F
13 °C	55.4 °F
14 °C	57.2 °F
15 °C	59.0 °F
16 °C	60.8 °F
17 °C	62.6 °F
18 °C	64.4 °F
19 °C	66.2 °F
20 °C	68.0 °F
21 °C	69.8 °F
22 °C	71.6 °F
23 °C	73.4 °F
24 °C	75.2 °F
25 °C	77.0 °F
26 °C	78.8 °F
27 °C	80.6 °F
28 °C	82.4 °F
29 °C	84.2 °F
30 °C	86.0 °F
40 °C	104 °F
50 °C	122 °F
60 °C	140 °F

chapter 10

My top 10s of everything!

Why did the teacher wear sunglasses?
Because his class was so bright!

My final chapter summarises a lot of what has come before with some fun additions to form my top ten lists of things that matter to us all. I'm always told never to confuse reasons with excuses, so here are some genuine excuses I feel work very well. What do you think?

Top 10 homework excuses

1. I ate it because the teacher said it was a piece of cake!

2. It's in my Dad's writing because I used his pen!

3. I ate my mother's chicken curry and was too ill all evening with food poisoning to do it.

4. Dad helped me with my maths, but I didn't believe his answers so I'm doing it again tonight.

5. I was at the Brit Awards collecting my award as 'Anonymous newcomer of the year'.

6. We had a power cut at home and only one candle between us.

7. I put it in the safe overnight and we forgot the combination!

8. It got ruined because I was fighting off a kid who said you were a rotten teacher!

9. It was IT homework and got mangled in the printer.

10. I went to hockey practice instead as I am more scared of the games teacher than I am of you.

Top 10 excuses for being late

It's a good idea to have a few ready-made excuses prepared in advance for when they are needed. You could even go so far as to write them down and tick them off when used so that you don't try one twice or with the same teacher.

Try using one of the tips below and see if you are able to get away with it.

1. I got right to the school gate before I realised I still had my slippers on.

2. My dog followed me all the way to school so I had to take him back home.

3. The postman delivered a huge parcel for me unexpectedly. I thought it might be educational, so spent half an hour prizing open the tape and staples.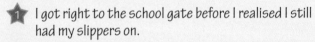

4. It is top secret; if I told you why I'm late I'm afraid I'd have to kill you.

5. My granny rang from Australia in the middle of the night and it would have been rude not to get up and talk to her for an hour, so I overslept.

6. There was no hot water at home and you've always told us how important good hygiene is, so I had to wait for it to heat up before I could take a shower.

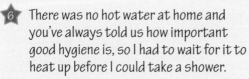

7. The dog swallowed the house keys so I couldn't get out of the house until Dad came home to release us.

8. Mum is worried about our carbon footprint so she made me walk the 5 miles to school.

9. The school insists that packed lunches should be healthy. I realised mine was made up of chocolate, crisps and cola so I had to go back and get some fruit.

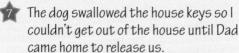

10. The bus driver was obviously drunk so I went home and waited for my Mum to run me in.

Don't go with strangers!

If you ever get separated from your Mum and Dad it can be very scary and that's just how your Mum or Dad will feel if you go missing. If it does happen to you stay close to where you got lost but always try to run into a shop to tell someone that works there.

If anyone wants you to go with him or her or tries to have a conversation with you while you are walking anywhere or offers you a ride or something, you should shout and make yourself heard and seen. You could just say you're busy or ring your Mum, Dad or even 999. Here is what you should do if it ever unfortunately happens to you.

 Always tell someone, shout to people.

 Never play in backstreet alleys or deserted buildings.

 Always take someone with you when you go out to play maybe a friend or relative.

 Always ring to tell your parents if you are going to change locations or will be later than you said you would be.

 Have a password that you and your parents have made up and only you and your parents know and if someone tells you that your Mum and Dad have asked them to pick you up, ask for the password and don't go unless they know it.

6. If you do meet someone that is acting strange always try and get a full description of him or her. If you see suspicious cars try to remember the registration number or write it down.

7. Never tell a caller that you are at home by yourself.

8. If you need help in an emergency always remember to call 999 – even if you are not sure whether you should or not.

9. If anyone does approach you say "No", get away and run waving your arms and screaming anything – "help, help, help" will do – as loud as you can. Remember someone can only hurt you if they can take you away somewhere and the best way to do that is in a car, so don't go near or get into anyone's car.

10. If a car pulls up close to you, it doesn't matter what they are saying, run away. Run towards the back of the car as that makes it hard for the driver to chase you as he or she would have to turn around first.

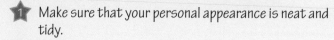

1. Make sure that your personal appearance is neat and tidy.

2. Always follow school dress regulations.

3. Never go in out of bounds areas.

4. Read your school rules on absences.

5. Respect the school buildings and property.

6. Make sure you are punctual.

7. Sort out how you travel to and from school.

8. Read your school rules on mobile phones.

9. Make sure you follow the rules on Internet use.

10. Make sure you know where cars, motorcycles and bicycles can park.

BEING A GIRL

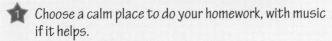

1. Choose a calm place to do your homework, with music if it helps.

2. Have a homework diary and stick to it.

3. Check your work before your teacher does it for you.

4. Don't let the TV rule your life. Record it!

5. Sometimes study with a friend.

6. Take short breaks every 20 minutes

7. Don't put off until tomorrow what you can today.

8. Do your best but ask for help with the rest.

9. Grab a drink and a snack before you start.

10. Presentation counts — keep it clear and neat.

Revision — the knowhow

Here are my own tried and trusted tips for terrific tests...

1. Draw up a revision plan well in advance but it has to be doable. Make sure it is realistic. Small bite-sized chunks of learning are more likely to get done that setting yourself three hours in one sitting.

2. Most people recommend revision in a quiet room with nothing to distract you but this can put a lot of people off as silence can be a strange thing for kids. I recommend some music in the background to keep you company and a drink by your side.

3. At some schools they do revision in the class but that doesn't mean that you shouldn't do some at home as well. School revision is an 'as well as' not 'instead of'.

4. For junior school exams you should start revising at least 2 weeks before — especially if they count for your report or grade card or your secondary school streaming system.

5. For entrance exams or verbal reasoning selections you will need to start a programme of revision about 6 months before and may need to pay a tutor to take you through it. Better than the arguments when Mum and Dad try to teach you.

6 Treat yourself to a biscuit and an exercise break every 30 minutes, I find 10 minutes on the trampoline or bike or a walk to the shop and back clears your brain ready to go again

7 Only revise one subject at once properly, don't switch from one to another.

8 Make notes as you revise. Write it down and you will remember it better. How many times have you read a page and not remembered a single word of it?

9 Get a set of highlighter pens. Use them to highlight important facts, words and phrases in your notes.

10 Invite a friend round and test each other.

Top tip

Never, ever write notes on your hands, cuff, ruler, rubber or pencil case. That is cheating and you will be disqualified no matter how well you have done. Just do your best.

Nearly all of us use the Internet but you have to be careful.
Here are some tips for internet safety.

1. Never open email attachments unless you're certain that they do not contain viruses.

2. Never click on links inside emails or instant messages.

3. Never use your real name in chat rooms.

4. Never agree to meet a fellow chatter in real life.

5. Never click on internet pop-up ads because they might install spyware on your computer.

6. Never use passwords that people can guess. Try not to use your pet's name or your favourite football team.

7. Never give out personal information about yourself, your family or your friends including your surname, your address, your phone number or even the town in which you live. Never send photographs of yourself or your family and never hand out PIN numbers for your bank account.

8. Never believe everything you read or see on the Internet. A lot of it is unreal and can be dangerous.

9. Never download pirate songs or movies even if your friends do.

10. Never be afraid to tell your parents or teacher immediately if you feel threatened by cyber bullying.

Burn a few extra calories doing little things while you work and play.

1. Take a skipping rope to school and do ten minutes of good old-fashioned fun — your granny will approve!

2. Got some chalk? Draw yourself a hopscotch grid and keep it up for 15 minutes to burn off the school grub.

3. Take a brisk walk round the field or playground. I know — it's obvious!

4. Walk backwards and you'll double up the benefit — if you don't fall over.

5. Practise high kicks or cartwheels — pure musical theatre.

6. Never use a lift or escalator — take the stairs and do it double quick (if teacher doesn't see you!)

7. Do your own pack up fast in the morning.

8. Start your own dance class at school, ballroom is very popular and involve the boys too. Belly dancing is good too if you've got the stomach for it!

9. Play cards, even on the bus. Be the dealer and stretch those biceps.

10. Grab yourself a yo-yo and start a craze.

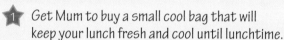
We all love crisps, chocolate and cake but they are very high in salt, sugar and fat and just not good for us. We need to be more healthy in our lunch boxes without them being tasteless or boring. Here are some ideas to keep lunch creative and cool:

1 Get Mum to buy a small cool bag that will keep your lunch fresh and cool until lunchtime.

2 So that you've got no grounds for complaint why not help with the weekly shop and choose your own foods as part of a healthy diet for your school time lunch. Just make sure you skip the aisles that house the sweets, biscuits and fizzy drinks.

3 A DIY lunch box might be the answer to relieving the boredom so offer to make your own lunch and then you may feel more inclined to eat it every day.

4 Try using different types of bread, crackers, bagels or whatever you like to eat at lunch as a change from the sliced bread sandwiches that you have every day.

5   Go continental and try other types of food e.g. cheeses, you never know you might prefer the lower fat cheese spreads.

6   We all know that fruit is good for you but if you don't always fancy that apple or banana. Try a few grapes, a small box of raisins or those small packets of dried fruits.

7   Cut out the crisps by replacing them with some plain popcorn or breadsticks, try only having crisps once a week.

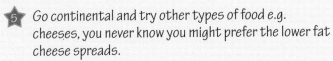

8   Freezing a carton of fruit juice the night before will act as a lunch box cooler and the juice will be nicely chilled by lunchtime.

9   Go for the reduced fat yogurts or fromage frais as they taste just as good.

10   The golden rule is to change what you eat everyday and that way you won't get bored but your body will still get the nutrition it needs and remember it is okay to have the odd treat like chocolate, sweets and crisps but just not too often.

1. Stand up for someone on the bus and you'll keep fitter and feel proud.

2. Chew your lunch twice as slow and use those face muscles.

3. Sing on the bus or school field, it will exercise the vocal chords (but not so loud as to annoy other passengers!)

4. Texting for an hour burns 100 calories — but that's no excuse!

5. Pick up litter round the school.

6. Clear up your own lunch mess and offer to help others if they are in a rush.

7. Iron your own school shirts.

8. Brush your teeth at lunchtime.

9. Laugh — exercise the chuckle muscles for half an hour by telling your friends some jokes and you'll feel the benefit.

10. Scrub up a vigorous lather in the shower and sing at the same time if you want to double up kicking the calories.

Exercise stops you feeling tired all the time, it helps you feel happy, it helps your body work much better and it helps you to sleep better. You should try to do about an hour each day of sport or activity but this doesn't always have to be through regular team type games. Try some of these for a 10-minute workout either at home or at school.

1. Warm yourself up with a whole body stretch.

2. Do side bends, keeping your back flat.

3. Put your knees forward and twist that waist from side to side.

4. Circle your shoulders forwards and backwards one shoulder at a time; make the circles larger and smaller each time.

5. Energetically march on the spot.

6. Try dancing along to some good fast music.

7. Do about 20 star jumps.

8. Skip on the spot for 5 minutes.

9. Jump clapping under one knee at a time.

10. Get a Hoola Hoop and swing it around your waist.

Boys love to impress with their prowess on the PS2, collections and detailed knowledge of Doctor Who. Girls like to impress by how unimpressed they appear!

So learn your lesson boys! Us girls:

1. Want you to listen, nod, accept and sympathise but never give advice or try to fix things.

2. Don't laugh at your jokes on purpose.

3. Want presents even if we say we don't.

4. Like lots of Valentines cards.

5. Like sporty types but not smelly types.

6. Hate bookworms or laptop loners.

7. Can spot a fake compliment a mile off!

8. Love a friendly smile even if we ignore you.

9. Hate to see the 'grubby undies' sticking out the top of your trousers.

10. Like a friendly text but not a late night nuisance.

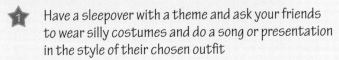

1. Have a sleepover with a theme and ask your friends to wear silly costumes and do a song or presentation in the style of their chosen outfit

2. Stay in your P.J.s all day and lounge around until bedtime.

3. Raise money for charity by doing something adventurous — a run, abseil or tug-of-war!

4. Go mad and do something you've never done before, join a new club or activity and make new friends at the same time.

5. Go to a concert or gig and dance all night.

6. Keep a diary for a month and lock it away for a few years, it will reward you with a good laugh.

7. Visit an elderly neighbour or relative with some hand picked flowers. It will make their day and may make yours as well.

8. Make a huge collage of your favourite photographs including your best friends, animals and holiday snaps.

9. Make the biggest Knickerbocker Glory ice-cream ever and eat the lot.

10. Tell your Mum you love her and smile all day — she will love you for it (and probably wonder what you want!)

Waste not want not

These days we are all told to slim down our waste and I don't mean your waistline. Research suggests that we throw away 3.6 million tonnes each year in England and Wales alone and here are some tips that will help you cut down on your waste in your day-to-day school and home life.

1. Take your food for lunch in reusable containers rather than wrapping it in cling wrap or foil.

2. Try drinking chilled tap water or buy a water filter jug instead of buying expensive bottled water.

3. Go to the local library and try hiring CDs, DVDs and books rather than buying them.

4. Buy products as far as possible made from recyclable material.

5. Give your unwanted toys and clothes to friends and family, nurseries or charities.

6. Sell any unwanted goods through free ads, car boot sales or on eBay.

7. Shop smart — look at the packaging that your foods are contained in and buy those that minimise this.

8 Don't reach for a plastic bag every time you go to the shop but take a reusable 'bag for life' with you.

9 Take your unwanted comics and magazines to your local doctor's or dentist's surgery or at least make sure they go in the recycling bin, there will be one near you.

10 Always choose refillable containers or bottles. If possible drink milk from returnable bottles that you give back to the milkman and not the cartons that go in the bin.

Useful websites

www.bullying.co.uk
The UK's leading anti-bullying charity

www.childline.org.uk
Help & advice at any time for any problem you have

www.talktofrank.com
An A to Z of drugs to avoid

www.nspcc.org.uk
Help for children and teenagers

www.beingagirl.co.uk
All a teenage girl needs to know

www.thesaurusreference.com
What you need, when you need it!

www.schoolhistory.co.uk
Interactive quizzes, worksheets & resources

www.activehistory.co.uk
Bringing history alive!

www.languagesonline.co.uk
Interactive self-marking language exercises

www.frenchrevision.co.uk
Tons of interactive French exercises

www.wikipedia.org
The free encyclopedia that anyone can edit

www.theaward.org
The Duke of Edinburgh Award programme

www.thescouts.org.uk
Adventurous activities and personal development

www.girlguiding.org.uk
Enormous range of exciting activities for girls

www.dayoutwiththekids.co.uk
The web address speaks for itself!

www.metcheck.com
Weather forecasts

www.youtube.co.uk
Share your videos with friends, family, and the world

www.bigwardrobe.com
The free, ethical, stylish way to recycle your wardrobe

www.redcross.org.uk
The voluntary organisation which helps people in crisis,
whoever and wherever they are.

www.webelements.com
The Periodic Table of chemical elements — just in case you
ever need it!

Index

The author

Starting a new school in Year 5 and moving again up to senior school at Year 7, meant Maddie Boyers had to face some serious challenges in being the new girl — how to fit in, knowing who to trust, getting to grips with new teachers, subjects, and routines. Lessons were learnt along the way and not all academic! How to join in sport and be a good leader without being bossy, how to follow the school rules without being a loner, how to look good in the uniform and how to stay strong and safe. Here she shares her own experiences with kids of her own age, in a unique book of tips, which will hopefully bring fun and comfort to the kids as well as their parents, during what can be traumatic times. Have fun not fear — school is what you make it. So as Maddie says "make the memories great!"